resourceful living

resourceful living

REVAMP

YOUR

HOME

with key
pieces,
vintage
finds and
creative
repurposing

Lisa Dawson

Photography by Brent Darby

KYLE BOOKS

This book is for my dad, John Kerman, who would be appalled at my wallpapering technique but also very proud that I can handle a drill.

An Hachette UK Company
www.hachette.co.uk

First published in Great Britain in 2021 by Kyle Books,
an imprint of Octopus Publishing Group Limited
Carmelite House
50 Victoria Embankment
London EC4Y 0DZ
www.kylebooks.co.uk

ISBN: 978 0 85783 919 0

Distributed in the US by Hachette Book Group, 1290 Avenue of the Americas, 4th and 5th Floors, New York, NY 10104

Distributed in Canada by Canadian Manda Group, 664 Annette St., Toronto, Ontario, Canada M6S 2C8

Publisher: **Joanna Copestick**
Assistant Editor: **Florence Filose**
Design: **Rachel Cross**
Special photography: **Brent Darby***
Production: **Lisa Pinnell**

*Additional photography credits on p.189

A Cataloguing in Publication record for this title is available from the British Library

Printed and bound in China

10 9 8 7 6 5 4 3 2 1

CONTENTS

A RESOURCEFUL LIFE

From fast fashion to fast interiors, we're entering a new era of being far more careful and considered about what we put into our homes. This, I can tell you now, makes me very happy. As a long-time advocate of repurposing and recycling what we have and investing in key pieces, I am feeling hopeful that both charities and secondhand stores will be first in line to feel the benefit of this move toward resourceful living. The recycling of interiors, buying less and buying carefully, is an all-round winner, limiting landfill and being kinder to both the environment and, ultimately, to our pockets.

Online secondhand auctions and marketplaces are a force to be reckoned with, whether you are selling or buying. But what should you look for? And how can you incorporate these finds into your home while at the same time remaining true to your own personal style? Social media has had a huge impact upon our purchasing choices, bombarding us with ideas, giving inspiration but also endless choices as to how we should style our home. Never before have we had so much interior content at our fingertips, and now is the time to use this influence to encourage more considered living.

Gone are the days of our childhood when we simply popped to the local department store for a coffee table – now we are thinking in far more detail about our requirements. Can I repurpose something from elsewhere in my home? What's my budget? Can I sell something in my home I've lost the love for and invest in an alternative? Can I multitask this purchase elsewhere around my home if I decide to change up my room? Is this piece going to work for the way I live today? Or can I adapt something that I already have? Considered, long-term purchases are the way to go.

I've been obsessed with vintage for a very long time. I've always loved mixing old and new – a style that is the backbone of my house decor – and it never fails to make me happy. I'd restricted myself to thrift shop trawling until about nine years ago when I decided that we needed a new sofa but were pretty low on cash. All the ones in my price bracket were small, barely deep enough for the kids to sit on without falling off, and all were a contemporary style. I wanted something a bit different, so I took to eBay. My first yearning was for a low-backed little Danish number, but my husband Joe wasn't having it – he'd been scarred for life by my sister's Robin Day sofa, which he'd always compared to sitting on a park bench.

Then fate struck – a huge, red leather corner sofa popped up. It was about eight years old and a Natuzzi, a high-end brand, with a very low starting price. The seller had a small account and obviously no idea about how to use eBay, as the auction was finishing at 3pm – certain suicide for a listing. Anyway, I sat outside school at pick-up waiting patiently – there were no other bidders. I sent Joe in a van to collect it from a third-floor apartment in the City of London where he met the owner, a very smart guy in his early twenties whose parents had given the sofa to him when he bought his first home. It was in perfect condition, feather filled and an absolute steal. I still have it now, although after three children, a dog and cats and plenty of sun bleaching it's not in quite as mint condition as it was.

My addiction to pre-owned furniture was set in stone and, since then, I've been incapable of styling a room without a bit of vintage. For me, it adds that extra interest, that touch of individuality which, in a world of trends, is so important when designing your home. We are under much pressure to incorporate shiny, bright new interior ideas, and this has created often identikit social feeds, losing that touch of personality we all dream of when planning our spaces. Thinking carefully about new purchases is an essential. Is it a good investment? How long are you going to love it for? I can tell you from experience, if it's a trend-based purchase, then generally for about two minutes.

The way that we live today will impact on the way that we live in the future (just ask Greta Thunberg). We can't do everything; it's not possible to be completely 'worthy' at all times. Much as we'd all love to be able to say that we buy underwear woven from recycled sacks, sewn by old women in the Outer Hebrides and flown to us by carrier pigeon, it's not really feasible. But what we CAN do is make our own small changes. And a good place to start is in the home.

Investing in new, well-thought-out statement pieces not only makes us happy, but is also a key part of building a home that suits us. By teaming these purchases with vintage and repurposed buys, whether big or small, you'll be making solid inroads into a resourceful and long-term way of living. And the side effect of this action? You'll not only be reusing treasures and saving them from landfill, but your home will reflect what you love. And in an age where we are bombarded with ideas and inspiration via our social media channels, this is a welcome bonus.

This book will guide you through the ways in which you can build a home that not only makes you smile when you walk through the door, but that is also adaptable to the way we live today – sourcing and repurposing to create a space that is resourceful but that also reflects your own personal style. And, most importantly, having a lot of fun doing so along the way.

LISA'S HOME: THE FLOOR PLAN

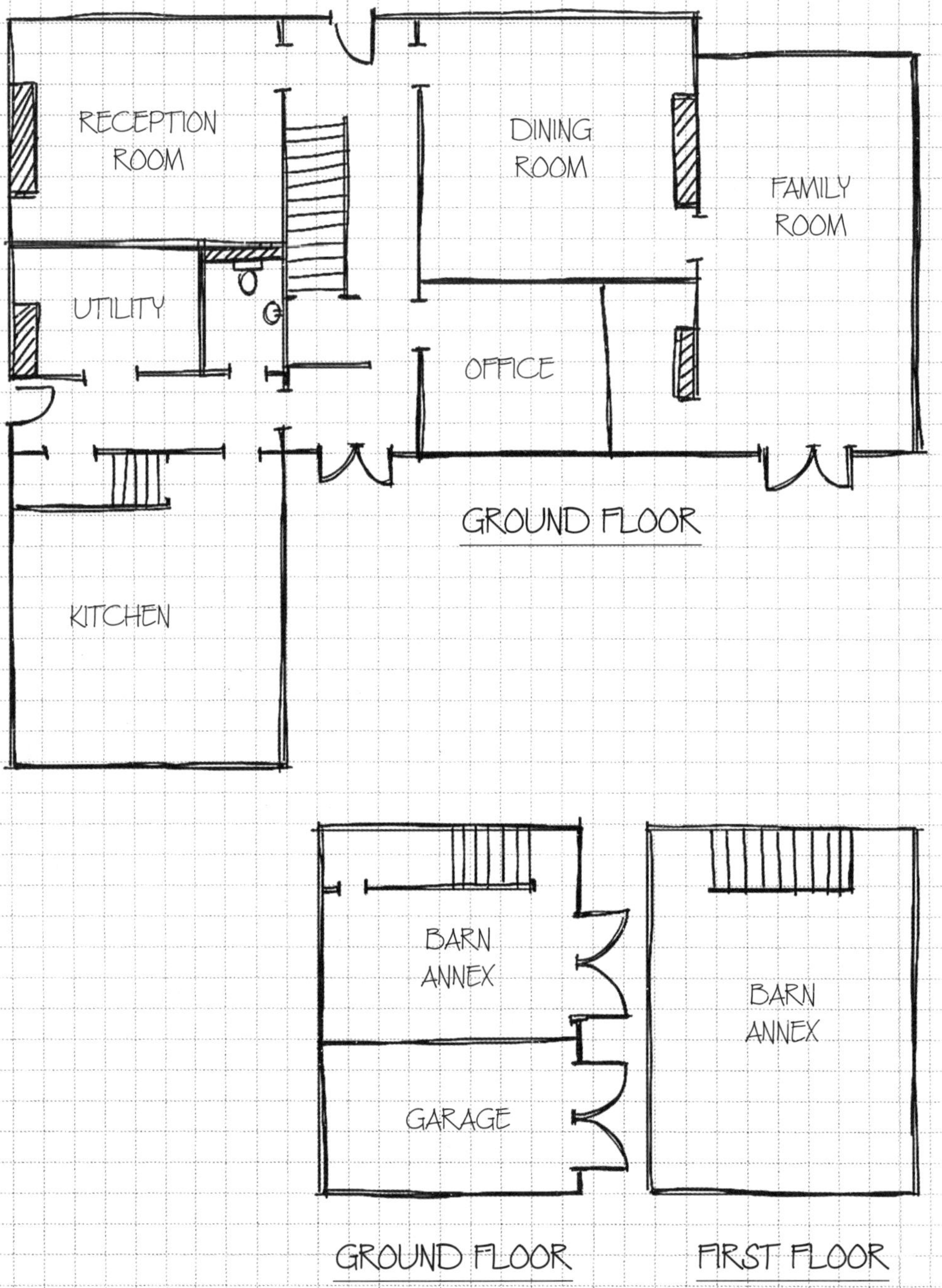

RECEPTION ROOM

DINING ROOM

FAMILY ROOM

UTILITY

OFFICE

KITCHEN

GROUND FLOOR

BARN ANNEX

GARAGE

BARN ANNEX

GROUND FLOOR

FIRST FLOOR

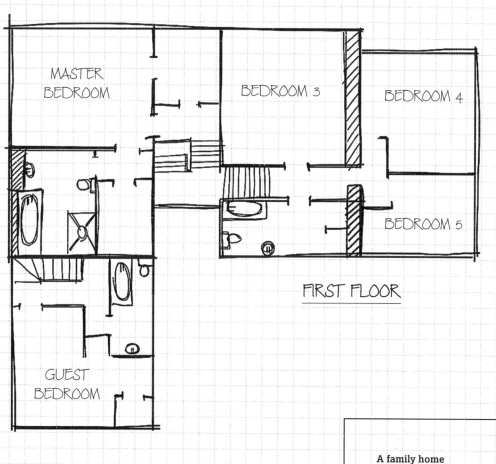

MASTER
BEDROOM

BEDROOM 3

BEDROOM 4

BEDROOM 5

FIRST FLOOR

GUEST
BEDROOM

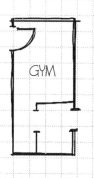

GYM

GROUND FLOOR

A family home

*Sometimes it takes a while to
figure out the best way to make the
most of your home so that it flows
correctly, and I think it's taken
five years for us to finally nail it.
We've gradually come to realize
how each room can be used to its
best advantage and now we have
a house that truly does work for us
as a family. We've maximized what
we have and multitasked spaces
so that they are flexible for the way
in which we live today. And, yes,
that does include a home bar in the
family room. Priorities.*

THE BASICS

The first thing to do in order to create a home that is suited to you and your style is to
get the basics right. Your home is your very own blank canvas and what you add to this
piece of interior art is what will make your heart sing when you enter.
Plan well and you're winning.

FIRST THINGS FIRST

Let's start by talking about how you are going to make your rooms work for you. The first step on this road to a home that makes you happy is to get the basics right, something that isn't always as simple as it appears. We want our homes to tick every box – be welcoming while still our personal haven, functional yet stylish, individual but with a nod to current trends and ideas. We want our spaces to feel cohesive; we want them to incorporate special memories, investment pieces, family treasures and thrift-shop finds that reflect our personalities. No pressure, people. Let's face it, with so much to consider, it's no wonder many of us falter in confidence when we approach the decorating of our own homes.

Getting your decor right isn't always easy. Over the years, I've gone through many phases in my quest to create the perfect space. My first major interior error occurred when it came to colour choices in the bedroom of our first buy, a new-build terraced (row) house that was ripe for trying out my limited decorating repertoire. For reasons that to this very day I cannot justify, I chose lime green for the walls and matched it with a lime green jersey duvet set. We chose a king-sized bed that filled the entire space, giving the overall reflective effect of making anyone who entered the room look like they were about to throw up. I have photographs of my daughter Ella lying on this bed as a newborn looking like a child of Shrek.

The surefire route to creating a home that is as beautiful as it is resourceful is to start by looking at the bones of the space. Every home has at least one lovely feature, whether it be a seven-bedroom country pile or a studio apartment. The aim is to bring out the beauty and make the most of what you've got. You might be lucky enough to have original floorboards or mouldings. You might have a large feature window or French doors, a wide expanse of wall perfect for curating art prints, or lofty ceilings that make the room feel bigger. Maybe there's an original fireplace hidden behind that shabby chimney breast? Start by making these bonus items the focus of the room. Make them shine – don't hide them away. Then work your room plan around these features. What you then add to this space will be the icing on the cake.

There are several things to think about when you're deciding how you will furnish and decorate your room. Sourcing items for your home shouldn't be an 'add to cart' process (although I have to admit to being an expert in this in other areas of my life, much to the detriment of my bank account). Taking the time to research and find furniture and accessories that you truly love, pieces that you'll use time and time again, is well worth the effort.

OPPOSITE: Accentuating the original door moulding by adding vintage books arranged in colour tones creates a feature.

My dining room takes advantage of every inch of space with floor-to-ceiling shelving that makes the most of the wall's proportions.

COSY NOT COSTLY

When I first started writing my weekly blog, I was inspired to do so by the hundreds of questions that I'd receive via my Instagram account concerning my obsession with thrift shopping. I had – and still have – an obsessive compulsion to trawl the local thrift shops in the search for the perfect buy to adorn my home. For many years, I've been stoically undeterred by the general faint whiff of mustiness that often comes from house-clearance furniture; the aroma of eau de old people emitted from 1950s sideboards has never stopped me in my quest. From wooden-framed prints of doe-eyed, large-headed children wearing pyjamas while fishing in lakes through to intricately designed 50-piece vintage tea sets, I have always had an addiction to what can only be described as the thrill of the chase. The older, the better, quite frankly. I'm talking interior finds, not George Clooney, although, let's be honest, I'd probably put him in my shopping cart if he had a Week 5 clearance sticker on him.

Making your home reflect your personal style is defined by the care that you take when considering what to put in it. You want your space to feel warm and welcoming; you want your heart to sing when you enter each room. This will make you feel happy and therefore enhance your life. Historically, we've been a society where more is more, but changes to the way we live today, to the planet and to how we approach purchasing means that we're far more careful and selective when choosing items to fill our homes. Less is more; it's about the quality and not the quantity.

*OPPOSITE: Outdoor-inspired decor is uplifting and mood boosting. **THIS PAGE**: A vintage tea trolley can be used both indoors and out.*

The first place to look when planning your space is, in fact, close to home – memories, family pieces, special moments that can be incorporated into the decor. I have a fair few pieces in my home that I've 'inherited' (basically stolen) from my mum. We lived in Hong Kong as children and I have a fabulous Chinese embroidered print on my wall that I purloined. A chest that belonged to my great-grandmother is in my bedroom, as is a green glass decanter that belonged to my great uncle. I love that these items can continue to be appreciated in my home. Handing down items not only makes your home look unique, but also means that you have pieces that hold memories.

There is much joy to experience when shopping vintage, for several reasons. Firstly, there's fun to be had in the searching. Need a new coffee table? Curating a collection of vintage glassware? Planning a wall of art deco mirrors? Scouring the auction sites and secondhand stores can be both exciting and therapeutic. Secondly, you're likely to secure the perfect piece for far less than you'd spend on something new, while buying something that is both solidly made and unique. The old adage, one man's trash is another man's treasure, is never more obvious than when you're trawling a thrift shop. I am always amazed at the preloved goodies that can be found, both from a quality and beauty perspective.

And thirdly, whatever you decide to purchase, whether a glass vase, a tea set or a vintage sideboard, you're saving it from landfill and thus contributing to the wellbeing of the planet. You are taking something that someone else has lost the love for and bringing it back to life, repurposing it and making a place for it in your home for years to come. Winning all round. But don't get me wrong. I'm not saying that your house needs to resemble your grandmother's, far from it. Key modern pieces juxtaposed with vintage finds work perfectly – mixing old and new reflects our own personalities while still giving our homes individuality.

It's all in the styling. A modern typography print above a mid-century sideboard looks eternally cool. Using vintage cutlery (or silverware) and glassware on your dining table setting alongside modern china and textiles makes the whole setup more interesting. A collection of vintage books placed in colour-toned order gives a contemporary feel to items that, on their own, can look a bit dull. It's the contrast of the pieces that gives your space the X factor.

OPPOSITE: Vintage accessories add interest. THIS PAGE above: This screen was a brilliant find on Gumtree selling site. Below: Juxtaposing a vintage lamp with a modern print.

THE TREND TRAP

I've seen a fair few trends come and go. Some are timeless, some hang around for a while and some are here for less time than it takes to boil a kettle. Due to the transience of social media, anything that is new, individual and exciting is filling your feed before you can say 'neon cactus'. Unfortunately, the very popularity of a trend is often its downfall, as once everybody has it, nobody wants it. Wikipedia defines the concept as follows: 'Trends often result from an activity or behaviour being perceived as emotionally popular or exciting within a peer group or being deemed "cool". A trend is said to "catch on" when the number of people adopting it begins to increase to the point of being noteworthy. Trends often fade quickly when the perception of novelty is gone.' Exactly.

It took me until I was 37 years old to have confidence in my own ideas and grow my core home aesthetic. Even now, I often veer off track by the influx of shiny new trends that I see in the stores and on my social platforms – it's like being tempted in a sweet shop. It's taken me a while to learn that when I launch myself at the pick 'n' mix, I should stop filling the bag before I actually feel sick. Sometimes it's hard to see the wood from the trees when your style is evolving. Or the fizzy cola bottles from the fudge squares.

So how can you make sure that you don't fall into the trend trap? The answer is to take them lightly. Add a touch of a trend – a cushion, a print, an accessory – but keep the bones of your room neutral. This means that you can take advantage of new colours and new ideas when they happen without having to totally redecorate your space. Look around your rooms and narrow down what your core style is. Think about the rooms in your home that make you most happy and think about WHY they do. Is it the colour? The light? The style of furniture? Focus in on what you really love before you jump in. Don't buy the jewel-coloured velvet sofa that looks great on everyone else's feed if your home is an ode to earthy tones. The focal-painted lofty high ceiling of someone else's Victorian villa looks fabulous, but will it look the same in your new build? Possibly not.

Most importantly, what goes into our homes has to be long-term sustainable. Take kitchens or bathrooms, for example. Or flooring, whether carpet, tiles, wood or LVF (luxury vinyl flooring). These are proper, hard-core, expensive purchases that you will most probably make only once a decade, if not less. Here today, gone tomorrow doesn't cut the mustard when you're dealing in a lot of hard cash. These items are the bones of your home, they need to be right and they need to last. Try not to jump on a trend unless you are 100 per cent sure you'll still love it in six months. Be sure to consider carefully before investing in the big guns. However, that's not to say that it's not easy to be influenced by what you see online and in magazines when it comes to making these decisions.

Trends make the interiors world go around; they're exciting, invigorating and inspiring. As a decorator who is constantly restyling, I'm always looking for new things to update my rooms with, and adding a hint of something new can be a good way of changing things up. The trick is to avoid introducing so many trends that your own personality becomes lost in translation.

OPPOSITE: A central tray on your coffee table is a great way to update the room.

Quiet Pattern   Abigail Edwards

CLEARVIEW

WHAM

interiors

SIR

TRENDS
CHECKLIST

---

1. KNOW YOUR SUBJECT

We're bombarded with new ideas from all sides – social media, television, magazines – so make sure you know what you are getting into before you invest your hard cash.

2. TIME IT RIGHT

Trends come and go like buses, so it's good to know how to spot them before you jump on and buy a ticket. Once the trend popularity peaks, it's everywhere, and once it's everywhere, the novelty has gone and with it the draw of the new addition.

3. CONSIDER CAREFULLY

Think about what you really love before you jump in and add the newest interior trend to a room. Focus on your core style and don't be influenced by the fact that everyone else has it – what looks good in one space might not suit your own. Consider why your home makes you happy and if the new purchase will fit with that ethos.

4. START SMALL

So you're smitten with the latest colour, the latest pattern, the one that's in all the magazines. Don't go all out immediately. Try it out first. Paint one wall pink instead of the entire room. Wallpaper a cupboard. Invest in a cushion, a throw, a vase, something small that won't break the bank. By doing this, by living with it for a bit, you'll know if it's truly for you, whether it suits your style.

5. THINK SUSTAINABLY

Your home and what you put in it has to last the course and that means that not only do you have to be able to multitask it in different rooms, but you have to really, truly love it. It's a long game, so consider new purchases carefully, particularly before investing in the big guns, aka the bones of your home: flooring, tiles and hardware.

6. BE CONFIDENT

You've thought carefully about it, you've done the research, you've tried it out. And you know what? You still love the trend. So go for it!

THE ART OF MULTITASKING

Choosing furniture to put in our homes should be a labour of love. The rule of thumb is as follows: only have in your home items that you really, truly adore. In order to make our homes resourceful and sustainable, we need to think about new purchases carefully – whatever comes in has to stay for a while. After all, we're trying to furnish our homes for life, not just for Christmas.

It has to be said that over the last few years, we've all become cleverer with what we buy for our spaces. Much cleverer. Gone are the days when we'd launch ourselves at a room set and buy every piece for ease, matching our coffee tables with our bookcases and our side tables with our television units. I am most certainly guilty of this decorating theme. Our first house purchase was a three-bedroom new build with an open-plan sitting room and kitchen diner, fortuitously (or so we thought) a hop, skip and a jump away from the local pine warehouse, a veritable treasure trove of every pine item available to man. We had busy jobs, no kids and we needed furniture fast. From bookcase to bed, from wardrobe to dressing table, from dining table to coffee table, from chair to mirror, every item in our home was pine. We were a house drowning in pine, in fact. In retrospect, we should possibly have put a little more thought into our decor but we were too busy drinking wine, going on mini-breaks to Amsterdam and having 5am finish, tequila-slamming, chain-smoking dinner parties with our similarly life-phased neighbours to properly plan our purchasing choices for the future. A rookie error.

Over the following 15 years and stuck with the ill-thought-out pine purchases, I made the most of what I had. I upcycled each item to within an inch of its life, painting, wallpapering, changing knobs and, most importantly, multitasking it. The console was moved to the bedroom, the dining table became a desk. The coffee table worked hard as an alcove display unit, and the dining chairs doubled up as bedside tables in the children's rooms. Each transformation made me really happy, knowing that an item that had lost its 'edge' had been repurposed into something useful. Bit by bit, this plethora of pine left the house, sold, gifted or thrifted over the years, to be replaced with something more suited to my own style. But what it taught me was that making your furniture and accessories work hard for you is an essential factor in making your home a long-term investment.

Any item of furniture that you choose to invest in should have the ability to be multitasked. Within reason, of course – there's not a lot you can do with a sofa aside from sit on it. But who says that a drinks trolley (or bar cart) should only be used for drinks? I have a few of these dotted around my home that I've picked up for a song in thrift shops, and not one of them is used in the way it was intended. One is perfect as a side table in the living room, and I've even got one in my daughter's room being used as a bedside table. My own bedside table is an old blanket box of my grandmother's, a piece that would usually sit at the end of the bed.

OPPOSITE clockwise from top left: *A display cabinet multipurposes as a bedside table; a wallpapered sideboard works well as a bookcase; a chair makes the perfect side table; and vintage tea trolleys have many uses.*

Look at what you already have and utilize it – try the side table in a different room, use it in a different way, take it out of its comfort zone and see how it looks in a new environment. Multitask what you've got – use a bench as a coffee table, a vintage display cabinet as a drinks cupboard. Don't hesitate to move everything about and try all options. A sideboard (or baseboard) is ideal for storing stacked copies of your favourite magazines and just as useful as a dressing table in the bedroom. Add a mirror and it's the perfect size for storing toiletries and makeup – unless you are an 18-year-old girl (my daughter), in which case you need storage the size of a small lock-up.

Make the furniture that you love work hard for you. Think outside the box when you're restyling a room – being creative with what you multitask is an effective and easy way to give your space a whole different look without spending any money.

*OPPOSITE: An IKEA kitchen cart provides plenty of storage for all of your bedside essentials. **THIS PAGE** left: Incorporate clever shelving for magazines. **Right:** A vintage tea chest is another great solution for a multipurposed bedside table.*

SHOPPING YOUR HOME

I like to describe myself as a transient decorator, which is a completely made-up expression but one that I feel suits me very well. I am addicted to switching things up in my home. Many is the time that my children have returned from school only to find that the living room is now the dining room or what they thought was a kitchen breakfast bar has become the dining table. Even when I was small, I was always moving my bedroom around, obsessed with the idea of creating a new space. My mother could rearrange a room faster than a professional remover, and I hold her solely to blame for my constant need to shift things around. Nowadays, with the constant barrage of glorious real homes and inspiration on social media, it's even more tempting to try out new positions (I'm talking furniture, btw). But as we all know, it's neither feasible nor financially viable to be constantly buying new things.

But fear not. There's an answer to this creative conundrum and it's called shopping your home. But what does this mean? Well, it's the simple concept of making your space look a million dollars at minimum cost. Instead of immediately dashing off to the store when you get the urge for a change, assess what you already own – reposition it, restyle it and give it a new lease of life. Simple.

Curate in colours (this is particularly effective with glassware and china), position a favourite artwork in an alternative part of your home, rearrange a shelf for an updated look. Moving a rug to a different space in a different room can transform the feel of the space. Switch over your lamps – try a table lamp rather than a floor lamp to create a cosy corner. Or pull together your favourite accessories for a coffee table display. Your home is full of things that you love – looking at them a little differently can promote a whole new ambience.

THIS PAGE: Vintage suitcases provide handy storage and can add interest to a space. OPPOSITE clockwise from top left: Coloured glassware; Fun touches; Lemons adding a colour contrast; Pops of green; Holiday memorabilia.

Keeping the base palette neutral means that you can add whatever you like to your scheme, making it easy to move items around the rooms of your home without fear of clash.

ADDING TO YOUR HOME
CHECKLIST

1. DO YOU REALLY NEED IT?
You may love it, but are you doubling up? Adding another beautiful chair to a room
of six other beautiful chairs might be pushing it.

2. ARE YOU JUMPING ON A TREND?
Remember that you don't necessarily want to go the whole hog – a touch of a trend is often
enough. Try the pink cushion first before the pink sofa.

3. CAN YOU MULTIPURPOSE SOMETHING ELSE?
Shop your home first to see if you've got something that will do the same job without the outlay.

4. WILL IT WORK IN MORE THAN ONE ROOM?
Equally, make sure that the new item is suitable for multitasking in more than one area of your home.

5. DOES IT FIT?
Think about the colours and textures that are in your home already and whether it fits
with your core style.

6. CAN YOU VISUALIZE IT IN A SPACE?
Buy with an aim – know where it's going to go and how you're going to use it.

7. IS IT IN BUDGET?
It's easy to get carried away when you see something you love but make sure it's affordable
before you jump in.

8. DOES IT TICK THE QUALITY BOX?
New purchases need to last – if you're buying vintage, check that it's all in full working order.

9. DO YOU NEED IT OR WANT IT?
Don't buy because you need to, buy because you want to. Don't rush to fill gaps in your home,
wait for the right piece to turn up.

10. AND, FINALLY, DO YOU LOVE IT?
The most important part of adding to your home is only including items that you truly love. If you love
it, it's meant to be. If you're not sure, then leave it.

STYLING
YOUR HOME

We want our homes to be welcoming spaces for friends and family, but also to reflect our own individuality and interests. Have faith in your creativity and instincts and you will create a home that is brimming with your own style and personality.

GO YOUR OWN WAY

One of the reasons that I started writing my blog was because I was always being asked questions about my home decor on my Instagram account. These questions were (mostly) about interiors – what I did, how I did it and where I got it. Over the last few years, I've found that there are several interiors-based questions that come up frequently. These can be narrowed down to the following: How do I plan a gallery wall? How do I plan a room? And finally, my favourite, should I *insert interior decorating activity*? Such activities include (but are not restricted to) go dark, go white or most frequently, paint my front door pink even though my partner hates the idea. To these questions, I answer the same – go with your heart, do as you wish, ignore trends and friends and don't EVER ask your partner what they think about interior decorating plans if you think they might attempt to put you off. My husband is a motor industry Brand Director. I don't tell him how to write a balance sheet, submit a forecast or examine an under chassis (totally made-up word – I barely know what my own car is). Therefore, the idea of him having any input into the front door decor is, quite frankly, laughable. Partners, know your limits.

Having the confidence to start making decisions when you're planning your home isn't always easy. We worry that we can't do it. We worry that we will make the wrong decisions, that it won't look as we expect it to, that we're not capable of trying new DIY or styling endeavours. We seek opinions as we don't trust our own and end up making choices that are more a reflection of others than ourselves. But guess what? You are a creative person, even if you think you are not. Because EVERYBODY has the ability to be creative; it's just a case of working out what you love and pushing your boundaries. Confidence in yourself, trusting your own instincts, is the first step toward making your home a place that you love.

Adding to our homes, making them resourceful and calming places, can be a very therapeutic task. For me, there's nothing more exciting than finding a piece of furniture that someone else no longer requires that is perfect for your home. There are several excellent benefits to this, the first and foremost being that you are perpetuating the recycling process. Did you know that the UK charity Emmaus saved over 4,000 tonnes (4,400 tons) from landfill in one year alone? If you have ever purchased a piece of secondhand furniture, then this is a very good reason to feel quietly smug. Secondly, in a world where we are bombarded by trends, adding something to your home that is individual and unique will make you stand out from the crowd. If you are restricted by a budget, then purchasing secondhand is good for your bank balance, and might even encourage you to get your creative hat on with a bit of upcycling. Plus, of course, there's an additional bonus should you be purchasing directly from a charity, in that you are donating at the same time. Everyone's a winner.

But fear not. I'm not promoting the idea that our homes should be purely vintage. I'm not expecting your homes to be an homage to mid-century or 1970s kitsch. Not at all, in fact. Seeing your perfect item in a furniture store and bringing it home is just as exciting. The thrill of the new purchase is equal to the thrill of the thrifted find and shouldn't be underrated when you're planning your spaces. However, buying

well-considered items, pieces that you are investing in rather than just dropping in the shopping cart, is an essential part of building a home that is fit for the future. Making sure that you truly love what you are buying – and not purchasing on impulse – means that you're more likely to hold on to it and not get bored.

Making the most of what you have is a key factor in creating spaces that work for you. No matter what area of your home you are focused on, being resourceful when deciding how to decorate or furnish will create rooms that are satisfyingly your own. Mixing up your look by using new, repurposed, upcycled and vintage pieces not only gives your home the individuality we all crave, but also meets a need for keeping our decor sustainable and long lasting.

Left: *Favourite memories pinned to the corkboard sit alongside vintage and modern additions.* Right: *A French table and benches juxtapose nicely with a Cesca chair and a worn vintage rug.*

RESOURCEFUL MATERIALS

If I were asked to name one thing that I consider to be the most important when styling and planning rooms, I would answer, without doubt, texture. Whether you yearn for a minimalist aesthetic, perfect symmetry or are heading toward full-out maximalism, bringing texture to your space is the icing on the cake of your room and mixed materials add those final details that make a room complete.

Incorporating a mixture of surfaces into your decor layers the look and adds interest to your space. Using natural materials such as wood, concrete or stone brings the outside in, and reflective surfaces, such as glass and metal, are the perfect contrast. Textiles – soft throws, rugs and cushions – bring personality and colour to a room while adding the essential cosiness factor that we all long for.

For a transient decorator such as myself, using multiple textures in rooms makes it easy to switch up the look and move things around. Seasonal changes are an excellent excuse for a swap about (although who needs an excuse?) and layering your look means that it's not difficult to completely transform the space by simply moving around and repurposing what you've already got. The aim is for your room to be warm and welcoming while still reflecting your own personal style – combining tactile layers and materials will encourage relaxation and create an aesthetically pleasing array of views.

OPPOSITE: Layering textures in the courtyard garden creates a warm and welcoming feel to the space.
THIS PAGE: The contrast of textures – wicker, wood, metal and tile – adds interest to this corner of the family room.

Hard: *wood, metal, glass*

Let's start with wood. Used for centuries to furnish and decorate our homes, it's the ultimate in bringing the outside in and can be found and used in a variety of tactile finishes. Mahogany, wicker, pine and bamboo are all easily sourced and add a natural element. This welcoming of nature into our rooms promotes a feeling of calm (although in our house of five, I admit this doesn't happen often). My first major vintage purchase was a beautiful teak Jentique sideboard, which quickly became the love of my life. Since then, I've sought out solid, well-made pieces to

bring this feeling of wellbeing into my own home. The mid-century era was renowned for its inclusion of natural wood products, with designers such as Knoll, Ercol and Arne Jacobson combining clean lines with a timeless style. And, of course, no vintage home would be complete without a set of teak deer. Bamboo and rattan epitomized the 1970s in all forms of furniture and accessories – chairs, tables, mirrors and magazine racks can be easily sourced to add a touch of boho.

From galvanized vintage planters to folding garden chairs, aged metal adds both character and personality while also providing the essential element of practicality – industrial-style furniture was made, in fact, to be both simple and hard-wearing. Metal pigeonholes or wire baskets are excellent for storing pretty much anything you fancy, and metal signage – French road signs, store signs or individual metal letters – can be used indoors and outdoors to great effect. Or seek out chairs, tables and light fittings that feature tubular steel.

I've collected coloured vintage glass for many years, picked up in thrift shops as and when spotted – I've curated them into tone, and my collection never fails to make me smile. Who says glassware has to match? The same applies to dessert and serving dishes, a regular find in the secondhand stores and often beautifully embossed or etched. And an old French foxed glass mirror above a fireplace shouts its history while reflecting the light around the room.

THIS PAGE: Marcel Breuer Cesca chairs, combining rattan webbing with wood and metal. **OPPOSITE:** *Vintage lockers are a great example of functional storage that still add individuality.*

A table for dinner is far more lovely to look at when set with a selection of mixed vintage wine and water glasses. Contrasting colours and textures create an impact.

Soft: *textiles, paper*

Never underestimate the difference that using textiles in your space can make. A flurry of well-chosen fabrics and materials can transform your room from ever so slightly boring to sublime while bringing colour and texture. Multitasking your favourite items is a no-brainer – seasonally repurposing cushions, rugs and throws makes the most of your purchases and ensures that you never get bored of the look. Those cosy woollen textures that were so warm and welcoming in your living room during the winter will have exactly the same effect when used around the firepit outdoors when the weather gets warmer.

Sourcing a secondhand rug is well worth the effort – they are often excellent value, and it's easy to have them professionally cleaned or even do it yourself. Moving them around can create a totally different feel to your room. Persian or Turkish rugs are an excellent vintage buy – the more threadbare, the better, in my opinion, adding character and colour in equal measure. Jute and cotton, dhurrie-style rugs add texture and practicality and can be layered with heavier fabrics for effect. Flokati rugs are a good (new) investment – a reasonably priced floor filler with the added value of providing some serious comfort underfoot.

Always check out the textiles section in a thrift shop. Hand-crocheted blankets or throws add a personal and homemade touch to your space with the extra cosy factor. Ditsy floral vintage sheets or pillowcases contrast nicely with plain colours, and if you manage to score a preloved patterned tablecloth, then you're winning. My sister has a variety of fabulous tourist memorabilia designs that she's collected over the years and uses regularly.

OPPOSITE: Books are appealing to look at, adding colour and interest to the space. THIS PAGE: A thrift shop crocheted find.

And let's not forget the joy of the vintage paper product. No home is complete without a book collection, particularly if they're old and secondhand in a variety of lovely colours (always the stylist). Paperback books look super effective lined up in tonal order and can be used for stacking on shelves for display. Or use the books themselves stacked horizontally as a 'shelf' for displaying accessories. Ditto to the coffee table hardback. Individually, it's just one book. A favourite selection pulled together becomes a focal point. Simple. Think outside of the box when planning your walls too. Memorabilia such as concert tickets and menus, or old maps – perhaps of the area in which you live or somewhere special that you've visited – can be framed and hung to great effect.

*OPPOSITE: Interiors blogger Bianca Hall's colour-coded bookshelf is a focal point in itself. **THIS PAGE** left: Vintage Penguin Classics are stacked high using an Umbra floating shelf.* **Right:** *A thrifted velvet bedroom chair sits alongside a modern patterned wallpaper.*

WALLS

If I were to work out how many hours I have spent decorating the walls of my house over the last four years, I swear it would fall well into the thousands. From painting to paper to artwork, there isn't a wall in our home that has been left untouched. Walls are there to be adorned, and although I wouldn't class myself as a maximalist, I am definitely a fan of creating impact. It matters not whether your wall is indoors or outdoors – paint and design can be just as effective outside as they are inside the rooms of your home.

I love a gallery wall. There are a few reasons why the random combination of art brings me so much joy. First of all, it's totally and utterly individual. No one else will have a wall collection the same as yours, thus making your display unique. Everyone wants to be unique, hey? We are bombarded every day with trends and 'must-have' items – curating your own personal gallery is not only a great way of pulling together the pieces that are hard to place, but it's also a weirdly therapeutic task. Believe me, this is true. I've done a few.

Gallery walls don't have to be super planned. They don't have to all have the same frames (although they can if you want them to – it's your wall after all) and they don't have to be all one style of print. Mix photography, thrift shop buys, typography, old family photos, limited edition favourites. And hell, why stop at pictures? Plates, guitars, neon lights – anything goes. If you love it, include it. There's nothing more interesting than a gallery wall filled with items and prints that are special to the home owner. It's the perfect focal point, whether your

*OPPOSITE: My staircase gallery wall is filled with favourite prints and memories. **THIS PAGE:** Picture shelves enable you to easily update your display whenever you feel like it.*

display is in prime position in the hallway or gracing the wall of the downstairs loo.

Wallpaper is another good option. Over the years, I've used many patterns in my home and they've always added that extra wow factor when walking into the room. Whether you go for one or four walls, it's a great way to inject your own personality into a space. It's easy to be influenced by current trends and ideas, but when you pick a paper, make sure that you really, really love it. Every paper that I've ever used has literally sung to me – each one has been a work of art on the walls.

For rooms with no obvious focal point such as a fireplace or large window, a feature wall of paint or paper can provide a base for the rest of your room to work around, an anchor for styling. They're also a great way to accentuate these features, drawing the eye to the main focus. It's a good trick for disguising the bits you don't love, too – a dark wall behind the television stops the tech from standing out like a sore thumb. Paint is an inexpensive way to do this and is easily changed if you fancy an update.

THIS PAGE above: *This wallpaper by Mini Moderns is the perfect backdrop to a collection of tonal glassware, while being a work of art in itself.* **Below:** *A contrasting paint colour makes your favourite accessories pop.* *OPPOSITE: Covered wardrobes prove that wallpaper is not just for walls.*

10

GALLERY WALLS

Pick Your Location

Any space, any size, any position – a gallery wall brightens and adds interest to a space that otherwise would be lacking. The aim is to create a focal point. Landings and staircases work well for this purpose – high-traffic areas that are often overlooked for decorating.

Frame Them

Custom framing can be costly so try other options before you go down this path. You can pick up standard-sized frames cheaply at retail outlets or try thrift shops, which often have an abundance of frames, both old and new.

Think Outside the Box

Who says a picture needs a frame? Use spring clips to hang poster-style prints or try poster hangers – a magnetic strip of wood along the top and bottom of the print hung with cord. Washi tape is a cheap and easy fix but one that looks great alongside alternative styles.

Curate with Care

Choose artwork that you truly love and makes you smile. Shop your home for other art that could work in the room you are planning – some prints look better as part of a curated display than on their own.

Juxtapose

Juxtaposing different styles of art and frames is what really makes your walls stand out in a crowd. Mix it up – from a vintage print picked up in a junk shop to a framed ticket from your first gig. There are no rules when it comes to what you put on your wall.

Position It

The fail-safe way to do this is to use a rug as a template. Move the artwork around on the rug one by one until you are happy with the plan. Don't be worried if you don't get it all perfect immediately – it can take time to get it right.

Be Consistent

The frames don't need to match but you do need to be consistent when you are planning your display. Mix up the styles, textures and sizes but try not to have big blocks of frames that are the same colour, and ensure everything is evenly spaced apart.

Hang It Up

Measure the wall so that you can pinpoint exactly where the display will be placed and transfer exactly what you have laid out on your floor onto your wall. Start in the bottom left-hand corner and work your way up and across. Don't panic if you go off-piste a bit.

Use the Right Fixings

My own rule of thumb is this: a heavy or glass frame will need a drill, A3 size (11.7 x 16.5 inches) or smaller is appropriate for a picture nail, and anything smaller or very light will be suited to a Velcro picture strip.

Have Confidence in Yourself

Be brave – you can do this. It's not rocket science, it's just putting some pictures on the wall, and if you follow the steps here, you simply can't go wrong. Give it a go.

FLOORS

What is on your floor is part of the bones of your home. Some of us are lucky. Oh, how we envy those people who inherit houses from previous owners, complete with beautifully sanded original boards or tiles, only needing to sweep or vacuum before moving their furniture into the space. I have never been that person. Think 1980s lino, water-stained laminate or cat-destroyed stair carpet and you're on my level. When we purchased our current home, the stairs and landing had been newly carpeted. Unfortunately, they had been newly carpeted in cream, so pale that it was almost white. It looked beautiful. Perfect, in fact, if you are one person living alone who never wears shoes in the house, doesn't own any pets prone to unpredicted vomiting or have children who make your stairwell look as if a dirty protest has taken place. We get what we are given when we move into a new home, but flooring is one of the biggest investments when it comes to making changes.

Making the most of what we have is the first step. Flooring covers a multitude of sins, but it can also hide a great deal of beauty. My sister, Annabel, moved into a 1930s home a few years ago and was accosted by a threadbare burgundy carpet throughout the ground floor. After considering engineered wood as a replacement and being horrified by the cost, she decided to grab the screwdriver and lift a corner to see what was underneath. Original block parquet spread through the entire space, needing simply a sand and a stain to bring it back to its original glory. Not only did she save a significant amount of her home budget, but she also restored and maintained the history of the house for many more decades to come.

There's plenty that you can do to up the ante in your home without having to invest in brand-new flooring and carpet. By looking at what you already have and being resourceful when thinking of how you work with it, you can transform what looks untenable into something lovely. This may be original tiles that can be regrouted and polished back to their original glory. Or perhaps a staircase that, once the carpet is ripped off, reveals beautiful treads that can be sanded and painted. Or particularly unattractive outdoor paving slabs (we've all been there) that can be jetwashed and transformed with exterior floor paint.

And if what you inherit is beyond saving, think very carefully about what you're going to replace it with. Once it's down, it's down and it's your own hard-earned cash that you've invested – try not to be influenced by trends and drill down to your core style before making decisions. You may be smitten with those patterned tiles now, but once the shine has worn off will you still love them? Will they work if you want to update the decor? These are important questions to ask before you take the plunge.

OPPOSITE: It's important to take a long-term view when deciding which flooring to go for – classic styles like parquet will stand the test of time.

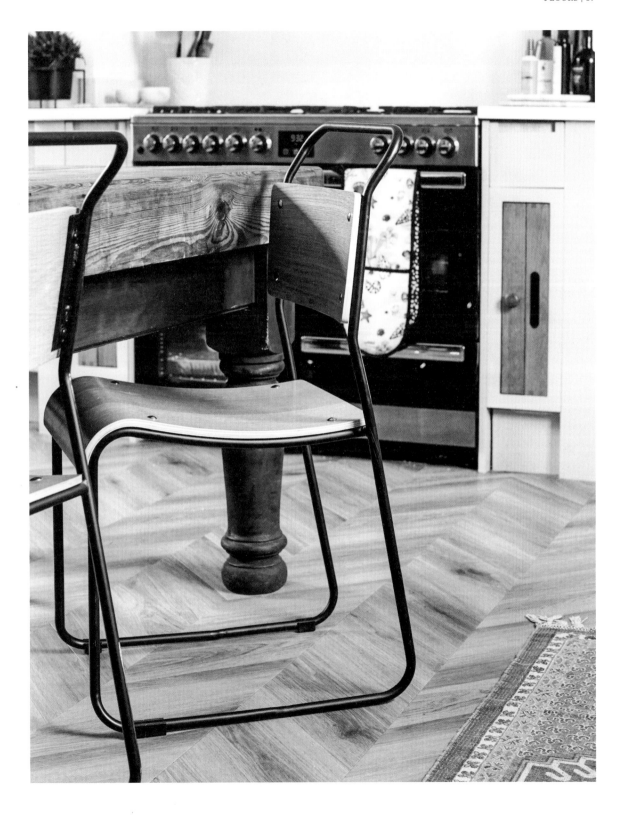

Ways with Floors

Let's start with an item close to my heart – the humble rug. I love a rug. My home is full of favourite finds, multipurposed throughout the house, used in multiple rooms and layered to within an inch of their lives. Perfect for when your floor is, well, less than perfect, they add texture and warmth to a room and bring that essential element of cosiness to your spaces. But where to look and which to choose? As with everything in your home, it's important to ask yourself where you're going to use a rug. Ah, a trick question. The answer is always the same – in as many places as possible. Going for a classic pattern or style such as Persian or Berber ensures that it's easy to flip between rooms. Natural materials such as jute or seagrass blend beautifully with almost all types of decor and are reasonably priced too. Layered up, you're winning.

Online auction sites and thrift shops are an excellent starting point. Vintage rugs are full of character and work brilliantly in nearly all settings, particularly when matched with modern or contemporary furnishings. The more threadbare and worn the better; they add character to your space. I once almost screamed in delight after discovering an old hall runner for £10 ($13) in a thrift shop, while the assistant looked on askance. Berber rugs are another excellent investment. You can find reasonably priced reproductions in retail outlets or there are small businesses that can source antique originals direct from Morocco on your behalf, depending on your budget. Again, this style of rug will work well in combination with pretty much any decor.

THIS PAGE: *Layering flooring is an easy way to change the look of your space – keep an eye out for patterned rugs or textures such as jute or seagrass.* OPPOSITE: *This vintage Berber rug is a timeless and flexible investment that will last for years.*

FLOORING
CHECKLIST

1. LOOK AT WHAT YOU'VE GOT
Before you invest in new flooring, strip back to what you have by lifting carpets
or checking under tiles. You never know what you'll find.

2. CONSIDER THE TEXTURES
Wood, concrete, tiles, sisal, carpet and LVF (luxury vinyl flooring) all have very different looks and
textures. Think about how you want the room to feel before you jump in with a big purchase.

3. STEP OUT OF YOUR COMFORT ZONE
Don't be scared of the sander. You can strip years of staining from floorboards by hiring the machine
and getting to work. It's a satisfying job that can yield much reward.

4. GET CREATIVE
If you're looking to make an impact, try painting the boards, either in a block colour or a pattern.
It's a great opportunity to indulge your artistic skills.

5. SWITCH IT UP
If you're saddled with tiles that you're not keen on (inside or outside), there are paint products
that will enable you to transform them simply by wielding your brush.

6. USE LAYERS
This is what will add interest to your floors – rugs will anchor your room and pull the look together.

7. MIX IT UP
Try several rugs layered alongside or on top of each other in different textures, such as wool,
jute or cotton, to add warmth.

8. MAKE IT FOCAL
Use rugs underneath tables, particularly in dining spaces, to create a sociable central point.

9. THINK OUTSIDE THE BOX
Rugs can be beautiful – if you've got a particularly lovely find, try hanging it on the wall instead.

10. SOURCE CAREFULLY
Don't write off a secondhand or preloved rug – sometimes these are the best finds. It's easy
to have them cleaned and the sense of history that they bring simply adds to your room.

LIVING

According to research, we spend on average a whacking 20 per cent of our time in our living spaces. That's a fair amount of lounging. I'd love to say that in my house this is equally split between chatting about current affairs, reading books and watching television but the reality is that at least 95 per cent of that statistic is spent arguing about what to watch on Netflix or who is going to sit where on the sofa. Whichever side you fall on, our living spaces are where we want to relax and unwind, a place where we can catch our breath and take some time for ourselves at the end of a busy day. We want to kick off our shoes, grab a glass of wine and a magazine, sink into the cushions, light a candle and feel like we are winning at life. Because, of course, we all are.

Making the most of our living spaces is absolutely essential. It matters not how large; whether it's a new-build home, a studio apartment or a period property, drawing the features out and creating a warm and welcoming room in which to feel comfortable is the ultimate aim. Sometimes, these features can initially be hidden. My own house is Georgian and when we moved in there were plain white roller blinds at the living room windows. I've always been a fan of roller blinds – window frames can be one of the most attractive parts of a room so it's nice to show them in all their glory. However, after a few years of living here I decided to redecorate the space and removed the blinds, only to discover that the original shutters were not only there in the sides of the windows, but also intact and working. It was an absolute bombshell.

Anyone who has original shutters, however, will know that they can be tools of torture – one wrong move and the bar comes down like a guillotine on unsuspecting fingers. There have been times when my dog Buddy has been almost wiped out by an unsecured shutter edge. Anyway, suffice to say that I was ecstatic about this discovery and when it came to redesigning the space, it was an excellent starting point for my plans. Whether it's a fireplace, attractive cornicing, large windows, a good view or good proportions, these plus points need to be shouted about. Making these bonus features the focal point of the room enables you to plan around them, rendering what can seem like a daunting process much simpler.

It has to be said, however, that our living spaces are sometimes difficult to get right. I've redecorated my own no less than three times. It's been flipped back and forth between a seating area and dining room more times than I can mention – I'm pretty sure it has serious identity issues. It's been eclectic boho, with hanging macramé and a cast-iron bulls' head for decoration. It's been pale pink, with a vintage plate collection sprawled across the wall. It's been a plant-filled, botanical wallpapered dining room. And, most of all, it's had more parties in it than Hugh Hefner's Playboy Mansion. But with slightly less scantily clad guests. Well, most of them anyway.

When you're planning your room, ask yourself questions before you start. How much seating do you actually need? Don't cram in a sofa and two armchairs if they're non-essential. What about storage? If you're a fan of the written word, you're likely to have books that need accommodating. How can you ensure that the room is well lit? Create cosy spaces by including different types and styles of lighting. By planning out

in advance what you need to include and adding what you WANT to include, you'll have a good chance of nailing it.

Creating a space that works for you can be a labour of love. We don't want to be driven by trends and we don't want to change it all within six months because we've gone off it. Our living rooms need to tick several boxes. They need to work as a practical space, whether we live alone or as a family. They need to feel welcoming and cosy. They need to reflect our personalities by portraying our own personal style. And, finally, they need to be resourceful spaces, incorporating carefully chosen items that are long-term choices that can work in other areas of our homes too, items that can be multitasked and repurposed.

Bring out your room's best features by making them shine, be that a large window, an original fireplace or a wooden floor.

Living room moodboard

Comfort is key
Create cosy corners by including soft lighting, artwork and plants next to comfortable seating

Inventive display
Use a variety of side tables as features in themselves. Stack books and add accessories to draw the eye.

Statement lighting
Go big or go home – a simple paper lampshade is a budget way to add impact to your room.

COSY TEXTURES

Big on greenery
Statement plants will add a biophilic element.

Contrasting fabrics
Combining textures and colours will make your room pop – velvet, wool and corduroy create a space that is warm and welcoming. Don't be afraid to layer these up.

Space Management

Let's talk about the first step in planning a room: formulating and managing your ideas. The worry that you won't get it right, that you'll mess it up, that you won't be able to make it look cohesive, can be a huge stumbling block. The answer is to start with Pinterest. It may seem simple, but it's an absolute guarantee that the end product will tick your boxes. Set up a Board and name it, then get pinning. Pin indiscriminately, pin wildly, pin loudly, pin like your life depended on it. It doesn't have to be rooms, it can be clothes, accessories, anything that appeals to you, anything that has the 'look' that draws. You might find that you're pinning mint green jumpers, you might find that you're pinning gold jewellery. Combined with your room pins, eventually, there'll be a running theme. Pin on the train going to work, pin when you're AT work (quietly, obviously), pin when you're sitting in the car waiting for the kids to come out of school, trying to avoid all the other parents. Why do this? Because by pinning what you love, you'll focus on your core style, even if you're not sure what that is yet. Eventually, you'll have a Board that will sing to you.

You then need to add these ideas to a moodboard. You can use an online app for this such as Canva or Powerpoint. Upload your favourite pins from your Pinterest Board and add in the extras – paint colours, textile swatches – but also pictures of products that you actually want to include such as furniture and rugs. I've been known to trawl eBay looking for the perfect photograph of a vintage Pieff chair (already owned) to place on the Board. What this does is focus your mind on the space. You might think that the gold side table you've pinned is an essential, but when you put it alongside the other elements that you want to

include, it might not gel. Add and takeaway until you are happy with what you see.

The next step is to clear the room. Dependent upon space, you might be able to do this physically but if not, clear out everything that you can. Strip those shelves, take down those pictures, toss those textiles aside. Work out the items that you still love. You may have had that Present From Cornwall sand-filled glass bottle for 20 years, but is it still relevant? Would it be better in the bin? Sorry, I meant box of memories. And that pile of old university text books (husband, take note) – is it essential to have *Motor Trade Management & Finance* sitting smugly on the shelf? Set into three piles. Pile one should be items that you love and want to include in the room. Two is for items you love but don't want to keep in the room. And, finally, three is for items that you no longer love and that can be taken with a hop, skip and a jump off to be recycled. As an obsessively transient decorator, I usually find pile three is quite large. Be ruthless – as Mufasa said, it's the Circle of Life. Send it off to be loved by someone else.

OPPOSITE: Narrowing down to what you REALLY love in your home will help you to create rooms and displays that truly make you happy.

Next up, shop your home. Look around for items that will fit the theme of your newly designed room. Art prints, vases, cushions, books – add to your pile with items that will fit the space. Don't just stop at accessories, either. The best furniture can be multitasked from room to room so take a good look at what you've got and do some swapping about. Not only is this a cost-free option but it's also a sustainable way of updating your space. And then, finally, style the room, one item at a time. Add your favourite item first – this could be a beautiful piece of inherited furniture, a favourite print, a special vintage buy. Work the rest of your items around it. By bringing the pieces in one at a time, you can work out when you are happy with the space. Add the layers – the plants, the textiles, the lighting – until you feel like you want to stop. That's when you know that it's done.

Transforming a space from basically boring to brilliantly beautiful is the BEST feeling. Taking a step back and reassessing can totally up the ante. Your home is your castle, your very own blank canvas and it's so exciting to think that you can make those changes, often with nothing more than a pot of paint, a bit of a rearrange and a whizz around your own rooms.

THIS PAGE: Trailing plants need little shelf space. OPPOSITE: Add to your room until you are happy with it – don't feel as if you have to completely fill it.

Furniture

My first piece of vintage furniture came from a charity sale and I've been a devotee ever since. It was a teak Jentique sideboard from the 1960s that was in such pristine condition that it still had the original label inside the felt-lined drawer. I paid the princely sum of £10 ($13) after literally throwing myself on to it at a local charity sale. These sales took place locally once a month, a hotbed of fabulousness comprised of all the items that the charity couldn't fit into its stores, barns full of coloured vintage glass, china tea sets and, most excitingly, an entire yard full of furniture.

I was obsessed, despite the fact you had to line up for an hour prior to the 10am opening to make sure that you got the best of the bargains. For my husband Joe, these sales were his worst nightmare. The only way I could get him to come with me was to bribe him with the promise of the pulled pork sandwich van that was always parked outside.

Ever since this fortuitous visit, I've been addicted. In my mind, there is nothing that can beat the excitement of stumbling upon a genuine find; the fun of checking the drawers to see if the teak joints are dovetailed, the realization that there's a rare maker's mark on the back of a cupboard that's hidden in the corner covered in dust. Bringing it home and back to life is both satisfying and therapeutic. The same applies to upcycling projects, giving an old, preloved and discarded item a new lease of life – making good the old is the way of the future.

Nowadays, we live in a consumer-led society, constantly bombarded with options for purchasing a new piece of furniture, but in actual fact, buying vintage can be a fabulous investment. It's easy to forget that the reason these pieces are still around today is that they were made to last and the quality is often unrivalled. Whether you give your vintage finds a complete paint job or just a repolish, it's hugely satisfying to know that you're repurposing something and perpetuating the recycling process.

THIS PAGE: A haberdashery display cabinet works perfectly as a storage unit. OPPOSITE: Interior designer Emilie Fournet has combined vintage furniture with modern art to great effect.

So how can you add vintage furniture to your home without channelling granny chic? The important thing to remember is to juxtapose your styling. Mixing vintage finds with contemporary accessories softens the look and adds personality to the space, creating interest and an element of fun. Think mid-century sideboard teamed with urban street art and you're on the right track. Let's take a few examples. Tea trolleys are an inexpensive addition to your home with multiple uses and can be picked up cheaply in thrift shops. I have a few in my home and they're multitasked to within an inch of their lives as side tables, hallway units and, most importantly, portable drinks trolleys. Add a few choice accessories and a plant and they're a focal point in themselves. Or a 1970s Danish sofa. Now, this can be a bit of an investment, but you're investing in a preloved piece that has history and character. Not forgetting, of course, the unwritten rule that anything Danish is always cool.

Repurposing what you already have is a clear winner when it comes to being resourceful in our living spaces. What looks as though it's lost its shine can usually be transformed with a bit of work. Bored of your bookcase? Give it a coat of paint, wallpaper the back and it's as good as new and twice as interesting. That old pine chest of drawers may have been hanging around for years but once it's sanded and re-stained with some gorgeous new handles on it, you'll wonder why you even thought about kicking it out. And if you're considering purchasing a new sofa because the cat has ruined the fabric (been there, done that), then upholstering in a glorious new fabric is far more sustainable than buying another. The rule of thumb is that if it doesn't move, it can be upcycled, and this is a true fact.

Finally, it's impossible to talk about preloved furniture without discussing mid-century modern design. Post war, the furniture style was characterized by simple, clean lines, natural materials and, most importantly, solid design and construction, which means there's still plenty of it around today with which to furnish our homes. Mid-century design also focused on bringing the outside in, which is perfectly aligned with the way that we live today: light, bright rooms with added greenery to layer the look. You don't have to look far to find plenty of examples of this style of furniture still available and it's an eternally stylish way to add to your home with preloved pieces that will last forever. Ercol, G Plan, Eames, Knoll, Breuer – good design will never go out of fashion.

Don't get me wrong – I'm not suggesting that your home should be an homage to years past, a museum of vintage. Investing in new, good-quality pieces will keep your home fresh and interesting – the trick is to make sure that whatever you add to your space suits your home, has the ability to be flexible and that you truly love it before splashing the cash.

OPPOSITE: Good design will never go out of fashion – vintage sideboards are eternally cool.

THIS PAGE: *Repurposed, recycled and new investment pieces sit alongside each other in the living space of my Barn Annex.*
OPPOSITE: *This Pieff lounger was a lucky eBay find and a flexible addition to the space.*

Storage and Display

If there is one thing that almost everyone suffers from in their living space, it's a lack of storage. It's amazing how much we manage to accumulate and how much of it feels essential. Every now and then, I like to assess what I've got, box up what I don't look at very often and store it away in the garage. Photo albums are an excellent example of something that takes up a lot of space but isn't actually a necessity to have out. Nice to peruse, though. I've got around this issue by taking out loads of my favourite photos – ranging from the really old family ones to the newer Polaroids – and posting them with washi tape on to the downstairs loo wall. They look cool, interesting and create a feature in a very small space, plus they're excellent to look at while you are 'otherwise engaged'.

Anyway, back to the living room and ways in which you can incorporate vintage pieces into your storage planning. The first place to start is the sideboard, an investment that will hide a multitude of sins and most often comprising drawers, shelves and a drinks cupboard. In my opinion, they're a no-brainer – why would you want to stuff your spirits in a kitchen cupboard when you can re-enact the traditional cocktail hour by utilizing it for modern-day use? Sideboards – also known as credenzas – swung into popularity in the middle of the last century when it was a sign of affluence to be able to dedicate a room solely to the joy of dining. Hugely practical, you can pick up originals in secondhand stores or on auction sites and they're excellent for multitasking. No longer just for the dining room, you can use them in the bedroom as a dressing table – providing plenty of space for even the most extensive array of beauty products – or as storage for books, games or linen.

I upcycled a long sideboard with sliding doors in my hallway many years ago and use it as a bookshelf. It originally would have been used for a china display but, in fact, it can be tasked for many uses around the house.

Another excellent vintage buy is the glass-fronted display cabinet. These would originally have been used for displaying favourite items and, of course, there's no reason they can't still be utilized for this purpose. Often spotted in thrift shops, they're ripe for upcycling and an excellent addition to your home. I use one in my hallway to display my vintage glassware collection. I painted it black and used some leftover wallpaper from a previous project to paper the back – it took no more than an afternoon to give it a completely new look. Multitask it as a bookshelf, a drinks cabinet or magazine storage – the best thing about these pieces is that you can easily update them with truly satisfying results.

Shelving is a practical and efficient way to create a storage area but it doesn't have to be expensive. If you're lucky enough to be blessed with chimney breast alcoves, you can utilize these to within an inch of their life with a bit of good planning. Most DIY stores will cut wood planks to size and it's not always necessary to employ someone to make your shelves for you at home if you're happy to give it a go. If you're looking to install something bigger, this can be a costly purchase. Before you jump in and invest in a full-blown premade shelving unit, it's worth getting a quote from a carpenter for a comparable price. Often, you can save in the long term by investing in a tradesman to create something unique and made to measure that

is far more suited to your needs. Plus, it's a long-term purchase and you're also supporting local business – winning all round.

Scaffold shelves are a good way to bring the outside in while still bursting with practicality. Again, easily bought at DIY stores, they're solid purchases that can be stained or painted depending on how you feel or how you want your room to look. If you're happy to put the legwork in, go on the search for old, used and gnarly ones with a bit of history. Google your nearest salvage yard, often the place to find some preloved scaffold gems. There is much fun to be had looking for the perfectly imperfect shelf, often with a side helping of other random finds. The best additions to our homes are the ones that have a story attached to them.

Left: *Arranging accessories in groups of three is pleasing to the eye.* **Right:** *A vintage display cabinet picked up on Gumtree selling site.*

LIVEN UP YOUR LIVING ROOM
CHECKLIST

1. CREATE FOCAL POINTS
Focus on areas of the room to draw the eye. Combine tonal colours to create an impact or curate a collection of similar objects such as glass or stoneware to add interest to the space. Or create a cosy corner by combining items of multiple heights and textures.

2. JUXTAPOSE OLD AND NEW
There's nothing more effective than the contrast of vintage and modern. A mid-century sideboard combined with contemporary art; a thrifted chair with a geometric cushion – the juxtaposition of styles and eras adds a touch of individuality to your home.

3. MIX THE TEXTURES
The best rooms have a pleasing combination of textures that layer the space and promote a welcoming ambience. Use glass, stone, metals, wood and natural materials to create contrast and use plenty of textiles in fabrics such as wool and velvet to add that extra dimension.

4. DECK THE WALLS
A gallery wall is a great way to display your favourite finds. Mix thrift shop oil paintings with modern typography; limited-edition prints with family photographs. It's the combination of these styles and memories that makes your home and your decor personal to you.

5. BRING THE OUTSIDE IN
No room is complete without greenery, and it's an easy way to add the biophilic element to our homes. Plants connect us to the environment outside and the inclusion of nature within our spaces brings the natural colour and texture that we crave when indoors.

6. MAKE IT PERSONAL
Adding accessories that remind you of happy times and favourite people will help create a space that truly makes you smile when you enter the room. Shells from a memorable beach holiday or a vase picked up at a Greek market – these items will add personality and bring joy.

7. MAKE THE MOST OF WHAT YOU HAVE
If you've got a high ceiling, a pretty window or fireplace, making these features the centre of attention will add interest to your space. If you have original floorboards, add in the character by bringing them back to their former glory and adorn with vintage rugs.

Bianca Hall's Home

Bianca Hall is an interiors writer, blogger, DIYer and art and design obsessive. Born in New Zealand, she relocated to Sydney, Australia, when she was seven with her mother, who decorated every rental house as if it were their own, always painting and adding personality. She started writing about interiors in a roundabout way, having bid farewell to a career in TV production. Wanting a creative outlet, she learned to screen print and started designing, hand-printing and selling art prints and textiles. Before long, Bianca realized that what she really enjoyed was interiors and homewares and decided to slowly scale her business right back. She started writing a blog about interiors, her absolute passion, and has never looked back. For the past 12 years, she has lived in a three-storey Victorian terrace in north London with her husband, their two children and Cleo the cat.

I first became friends with Bianca four years ago after seeing her collection of statues on her Instagram feed and discovering that she was a fellow fan of the iconic religious image. Her home reflects her unique take on laid-back luxe and her core style remains constant: playful, urban, grown-up glamour, new mixed with vintage and high-end with high street. Whether it's an Ikea hack or an eBay find, she has always been drawn to sourcing pieces that you won't find anywhere else. Initially that came about for financial reasons, but as the years went by, it became less about money and more about preference.

OPPOSITE: Investment art sits perfectly alongside Bianca's collection of iconic religious statues.

Why do you furnish your home resourcefully?

I just love the mix of old and new – it gives a space a layered look and so much more personality. The idea that you've found something really unique that you won't see anywhere else always excites me. Vintage has history, individuality and a timeless quality, plus you won't see the same thing plastered all over Instagram! A bit of vintage in every room, whether it's a big piece of furniture, a lamp or a smaller accessory elevates a space in a way that new pieces just can't.

Your living space is a feast for the eyes! What is your favourite piece within this space?

That's like asking me to choose a favourite child! It's a toss-up between my Lucite trolley that I currently use as a side table and my Arkana dining chairs. Both were very lucky eBay finds and I can't imagine ever parting with them. The vintage dealer I bought the trolley from was loath to part with it for the price I paid – I think he was as shocked as I was. I wasn't even looking for dining chairs when I found my original Arkana set. I was searching for an oval dining table, and they were included in a listing for a homemade oval MDF table. The person selling them didn't list the brand, but I could see the stamp on a chair base in one of the photos, so I snapped them all up.

The wall-hanging sideboard is a DIY project – what inspired you?

I had the idea of using kitchen wall cupboards as a cheap way of creating a sideboard in our dining room so I had a sprayed MDF top made by a local joiner. For many years, it was just a very simple storage piece. I had the idea of adding the stepped panels to the doors having seen images of similar sideboards on Instagram. I had the MDF cut to size based on the door size. Then it was simply a case of gluing the pieces together, then moving on to the doors, caulking and painting. It's probably the thing I get asked about most in the whole house. It was actually an incredibly easy thing to achieve, but it's elevated the piece so much.

Where do you shop if you're looking for something unique?

Due to the fact I work from home and have a family, I don't get to do much vintage trawling, so I almost always tend to shop online. eBay is still a brilliant place to track down good vintage items and my number one starting place – there are great bargains to be found if you have the patience. I also follow lots of vintage dealers on Instagram. Online shops such as Vinterior and Pamono are also well worth a look.

OPPOSITE: *Bianca's stunning sideboard is a clever IKEA hack. The wall panelling is also a DIY project and elevates the space.*

What are your top three styling tips for shelves and bookcases?

1. First, take literally everything off – it's important to start with a completely blank canvas. Then position the largest and tallest pieces first. Usually I wouldn't place them centrally, but it depends on the piece and the space.

2. Go in with all of the smaller pieces. Piles of design books are an excellent styling tool – I would use two or three – and make sure that they are different sizes, the largest at the bottom. Place something decorative on top, whether it's an ornament or a scented candle.

3. Plants in interesting pots are always a winner. Keep standing back and checking how everything looks, moving things around until it feels right, looks balanced and flows nicely.

Have you got any tips for incorporating vintage into your home?

Unless you can afford to go super high-end, mix it up with some modern pieces to stop your home looking like the land that time forgot. It's okay to have a seventies coffee table with a modern sofa, a fifties side table with a super-contemporary lamp – it's the mix that makes it interesting!

You have lots of beautiful art in your home. Do you have any display tips?

My husband and I have collected art together over the past 17 years. Most pieces are joint decisions, especially for higher-priced pieces, which is a good idea. There is no point in spending lots of money if your other half hates it. We have bought at auction, direct from galleries and direct from artists. Ed has been a skater since he was a child and has always collected skateboards. Supreme have always done artist collaborations, including two collaborations with Damien Hirst – we have a set of three spin decks hanging in the hall, and countless other artist collaboration decks hanging throughout the house. He's particularly passionate about only buying decks from respected skate brands and not just shops jumping onto the 'skateboards are cool' bandwagon. I'm pretty sure he could write a book on the topic and the meaning and reasons behind each and every single one of the many boards he has!

I prefer big pieces of art to lots of small pieces, especially in the living room where I like it to feel calm. We have one large piece on the chimney breast and one large piece on the wall opposite behind the sofa in the living room. In the dining room, we only have art on one wall – a grid of nine smaller prints in matching frames with a block of colour painted behind them to unify them and give the illusion of one large piece. This is also a great trick for making art look larger than it is. We also have a Grayson Perry Tate Modern silk scarf framed in the hallway. Again, this is a great way of creating a large piece of art. The framing is expensive for large pieces, but it's worth investing in, as it will last indefinitely. I love gallery-style frames – simple black or white frames with a deep rather than flat profile, and float mounting where appropriate always looks brilliant.

Find Bianca online @frenchforpineapple
www.frenchforpineapple.com

OPPOSITE clockwise from top left: *The Arkana chairs were a lucky eBay find; vintage statues draw the eye; a simple side table is an ideal base for this vignette; and a neutral wall shade means that Bianca's art collection can shine in the hallway.* OVERLEAF: *Bianca's home is the perfect combination of well-thought-out vintage and modern luxe.*

Lighting

When it comes to styling any space, lighting is one of the most important factors in the decision-making process. The way that you light up your home can make or break a room and is one of the most common mistakes that people make when planning. The right glow can create the atmosphere you are looking for, whether it is a well-lit kitchen or a cosy corner. I've always had a bit of an obsession with low-level lighting. I love the way it can change the look of a room at the flick of a switch. If it were up to my husband, we would have full-blown overhead lighting permanently in every room – I've lost count of the times he's walked in and upped the dimmer switch, bathing me in 70-watt glory. This trait is particularly irritating when we have dinner parties. I deck the table with softly glowing candles and lower the lights, causing him to immediately proclaim that he can't see his food and rush to whack them up, our guests and their beef bourguignon left looking like startled rabbits in the headlights. So annoying.

Subtle lighting is generally the way forward when it comes to areas made for relaxation. The central overhead light is an essential but needs to look just as good switched off as it looks when it is on. Choosing the right ceiling light is so important when you are planning the style of your space and it's often an area that is worth a bit of investment. It's part of the bones of your home, so sourcing a central light is a good opportunity to include something a little different, perhaps even vintage (although make sure that you have any vintage light purchases properly checked by an electrician prior to installation). Go with what you love when making these choices, but remember that your room size will have a lot to do with what you can pick. High ceilings can take big fixtures; small rooms will struggle.

Living in areas that are properly lit can really affect our mood. Research shows that people who worked in spaces with lots of windows are more likely to sleep better, exercise more and have more positive energy than those who don't. We take natural daylight for granted but not all rooms have windows that are big enough for us to be able to feel the benefit. Therefore, it's important that we have plenty of lights in our home so that we can make sure we don't lose out on this essential mood booster. The average-sized living room needs at least four light sources, plus an overhead light. The type of light can vary depending on how we want to feel or what we want to use the space for – a study area will require a much brighter light than a corner in which we want to relax. It's really important that you think hard about how you want that space to make you feel.

OPPOSITE: Make the most of the natural light that your home affords. Low lighting will create a welcome ambience and bring a cosy feel to your space.

The right table light can create the perfect ambience. Dark corners are not conducive to relaxation and can feel dull and unwelcoming. Large shades reflect and expand the light to make the space shine and encourage guests to feel at home. Go for statement, mixing textures and tones to suit your room. Use a matching pair if you like the symmetrical look or mix them up.

Another tip is to use varying heights of lighting. Floor lamps are a great way to create a focal corner – they also work brilliantly if you have an L-shaped sofa and no space for a side table. Place the lamp behind the seating area for maximum effect. Being able to adjust and focus the light where it's needed is an excellent benefit. In comparison, spot lamps are ideal for dressing tables or bedsides, enabling you to focus the light exactly where it's required. They can work in almost any room, from a kitchen corner to a shelf, highlighting favourite accessories or books.

Most importantly, don't forget that you can completely switch the look of your rooms by multitasking your lighting and moving it around. One of the quickest and easiest ways to revamp a room is by swapping the lamps – any space can be transformed by changing the focus and levels of the lighting you are using. Swap the floor lamp for a side table and low-level lamp for a softer look, or create a cosy corner by using a focused reading lamp alongside a chair and side table.

THIS PAGE above: *A large table lamp creates a cosy corner to relax in.* Below: *This vintage church chandelier makes a statement.* OPPOSITE: *Multi-task the lighting around your home by trying it in different spaces.*

DINING

There is nothing that brings people together more than gathering around the table for a good meal. Whether your dining area is part of your kitchen, an open-plan space, a separate room or simply a corner of your home, it's a place to meet, chat and catch up whether that be with family or friends; it is a place to feel relaxed and happy. And, of course, most importantly, it's a place to eat. In the words of Oscar Wilde, 'after a good dinner, one can forgive anybody, even one's own relations.' As someone with a large extended family, all of whom are lovers of gastronomy, I can confirm this to be a true fact.

Many of my best memories are of long, lazy hours spent around the dining table. We have a Kerman family tradition that goes back to my childhood in Hong Kong. It was madly hot in December and the idea of slaving over a stove was extremely unappealing so my dad – always one to try something new – barbecued the Christmas turkey on the balcony. When we moved back to England, the tradition continued and has been passed on to my husband Joe. As a man who barely uses the toaster and doesn't know how to turn the hob on, this is the only cooking task that he undertakes all year, so he takes it very seriously. It's always a big event and part of the excitement of planning for the big day.

But be assured, your dining room decor is as important as what you put on the table. I come from a family of obsessive table decorators. Both my mum, my sister Annabel and my sister-in-law Natasha can only be described as Olympic standard when it comes to styling any table that is to be used for a group meal. The often mooted idea of simply

chucking a place mat, cutlery and a bottle of ketchup on the table is met with what can only be described as abject horror. In our family, the benchmark is high and you have to be in it to win it. It's all or nothing. If your fully set table doesn't get at least a gasp of awe, then you must consider yourself a failure and try harder next time. Ruthless.

One of my favourite things to do is to prepare my dining room for a meal. It doesn't matter whether it's a dinner party for 16 or simply a family meal with my husband and kids – just adding the personal touch makes it an event. Lighting, ambience and a warm welcome make what could just be an eating area into a relaxed, social and appealing space. In fact, I approach the way that I plan my dining space the same way as I plan the rest of my home – by incorporating things that I love, things that make me happy. This applies to the furniture I choose, the textiles I add, the accessories I use, right through to the way that I display the meal on the table.

Planning this space is also a really good opportunity to get your creative head on. It's easy to make your dining area look beautiful by working with what you already have and repurposing items in your home – greenery from the garden for decoration, old pieces of vintage fabric for napkins, handmade table place settings. These are all simple ideas that anyone can do with a little time and patience – I'm not a particularly creative person but it's therapeutic and fun to try something new, especially when it creates an impact. Lighting a candle and adding a vintage wine glass can make the most boring meal more interesting.

However big your dining space, it's important to get this area to work for you and your needs. It may be that this area is multitasked as an office or used as a homework space. Storage is an essential factor in working out what you incorporate and how you do it. There are plenty of approaches to this. You may like to have your favourite pieces of china or glassware as a focal point, positioned in a glass cabinet. Or you might prefer to invest in a sleek, stylish sideboard unit to hide it away, or have it displayed for all to see on a vintage shelf. You could even incorporate a drinks trolley for social gatherings. Whichever route you take, there's plenty to consider when you're planning how it will work.

Wherever you dine, your space can be taken up a notch with a simple table setting and decoration ideas that will make every meal a special one.

Dining moodboard

STATEMENT
LIGHTING

Re-homed pieces
Thrifted finds in natural materials bring both personality and interest to your dining space.

Creative repurposing
Multitask your furniture – here, a filing unit has been repurposed as a china and glass display cupboard to show off favourite pieces.

TONAL
ACCESSORIES

Everyday practical

Your dining table has multiple uses so go for seating that can be flexible. Benches are excellent for accommodating extra guests, and juxtaposing different styles of seating combines the textures.

Personal style

By adding what you love to your shelves and displaying things that mean something to you, your space will make you happy.

Your dining space offers plenty of opportunity to incorporate favourite vintage finds, particularly pretty tableware – mix patterns and sizes for impact.

Furniture

Over the last century, the way that we use our homes to gather and eat has changed. In Victorian times, a separate dining room was the norm – the formality of eating was a big event. As times went by, both our working lives and the way that we lived changed beyond recognition and newer homes were far more likely to be open-plan or the dining space located close to the kitchen for ease and quickness of meals. Eating was no longer a big event (witness the advent of the ubiquitous microwave meal), more functional and essential than an experience to be savoured. However, in recent times there has been a move back toward the social dining space – dinner parties and gatherings – as we all start to relish the opportunity to take pride and joy in our homes by sharing them with others. Social media has played a large part in the democratization of design in our homes and we are now more confident and enthusiastic about trying out our own ideas and finding our core style when decorating our spaces. Basically, we want to show them off. And who can blame us?

The first step toward a dining space to be proud of is to curate and source the perfect combination of furniture. Let's start with the dining table. Work out the maximum amount of people that you need to accommodate for a meal on a daily basis. If you're lacking space, you don't need a table for six if there are only two of you 99 per cent of the time. There are some excellent extendable options to be considered – from a mid-century perspective, this style of table was very popular, often folded down and placed in the corner for everyday use. You can source these secondhand very easily on eBay and other auction sites, or try house-clearance warehouses where

they are often in abundance. If you have the room for something bigger, then it's worth spending some time to find something that will last the course. Long French tables hold their value and are a good investment, as well as being steeped in history and extremely hard-wearing. Try taking a second look at what you already have. You might have a table of the right size but not the right look – a hand sander, wood stain or a pot of paint can transform it into something special in a few hours. Or if you (or a partner or friend) are handy with the toolbox, go for the ultimate in resourceful decor – make one yourself with scaffold boards and trestles.

Now add some seating. If you've chosen a vintage table, then juxtaposing this with a selection of more modern chairs looks really cool. Unless you've got a huge dining space, you don't need loads. If you're not a regular host or hostess, then you can multitask other chairs from around your home if required. Benches are excellent for this purpose and enable you to fit more people around the table by squeezing them in for a party group, plus they're perfect for multitasking as coffee tables or hallway decor when they're not needed. Mix it up. Use different types of chairs picked up as and when you spot them – spend time sourcing your perfect selection and upcycle them if they're looking a big drab with a lick of paint.

OPPOSITE: Who says everything has to match? It most definitely does not. Mix textures and add greenery to create a dining space you can enjoy.

The right storage is essential. Old glass filing units make for perfect display cabinets to show off your favourite pieces of china or glassware – in my own home I have a vintage cupboard that I use for this task, to great effect. Glass display cabinets are also excellent for this very purpose. Sideboards were designed to be stacked full of china ready to serve and are excellent space savers for your kitchen cupboards when your dining space is open plan. Bookcases aren't just for books – they offer easy access for plates and dishes to go straight to the table and can be upcycled in paper and paint to make them stand out. I could go on, but you get the gist. Any type of storage or display is fair game when you're planning your room – it's all about looking at it in a different way.

And, finally, every dining space needs a retro drinks trolley. Whether it's a floral fifties trolley originally used for tea and cakes or an eighties smoked glass gold-framed beauty, stack it with your favourite drinks, add a plant, some cool accessories and you're ready to party. Job done.

OPPOSITE: An old filing cabinet has been repurposed to provide storage for vintage glassware and thrift-shop finds.
THIS PAGE: Don't let your vintage china gather dust – make every dining experience a special event.

Storage and Display

THINK OUTSIDE THE BOX

Your dining storage doesn't have to be traditional. Old glass display cabinets, shelving units, linen cupboards or vintage larders work brilliantly in a modern setting. If you're short of space, a sideboard is your homeboy. Possibly the most practical of dining furniture, these often have shelves for china, cutlery drawers and drinks storage.

ASSESS WHAT YOU HAVE

Shop your home to see if you have anything that is suitable for purpose. Those old shelves that were used for toys could be a perfect china display unit once sanded and upcycled. A blanket box can double up as textile storage, and a side table as a drinks bar. Or get creative – hang IKEA cupboards on the wall

like Bianca Hall (see page 83) for a unique take on a modern sideboard.

BE PRACTICAL

If there's only two of you, the likelihood is that you won't need a ten-seater table taking up all the room – think about one that can be extended when needed or scour the thrift shops for an upcycle project. If you have storage or a garage, have a piece of wood cut to size that can be placed on top of a smaller table when required, a quick and easy way to feed a crowd.

MIX IT UP

New chairs mixed with old favourites make your dining space individual and add personality. Upcycle what you have, and always keep an eye out on auction sites or in thrift shops for additions. Multitask your chairs around the house so that you can bring them to the table when needed for larger groups.

ADD LAYERS

Introduce texture with a pretty tablecloth or two layered on top or be resourceful by utilizing a single plain sheet for a large setting (this can be dyed to suit your colour theme). Check out the vintage fabric in your local thrift shop. It's a great place to source remnants – plain or patterned – that you can use as napkins, tied with twine or ribbon.

BRING THE BEAUTY

Using vintage china and tableware not only looks beautiful but is also resourceful – there's nothing

THIS PAGE: Old wine-making bottles. OPPOSITE left: Emilie Fournet's vintage teapots. Right: Everyday china and glassware.

better than setting a table with pieces that have a history. Pick your favourite florals or designs, layering with your normal plain dinnerware for that vintage/modern mix. And don't bypass the vintage tea sets – it's far nicer being served your after-dinner coffee in a glorious mid-century teacup.

ADD THE EXTRAS

Vintage glassware is easily sourced and is often far more intricate than contemporary pieces. Team your place settings with a selection of thrift-shop finds – etched water, wine and liquor glasses look fabulous when mixed, and look out for vintage decanters to bring that bit of edge to your bar cart. I've been collecting vintage cutlery – cheese knives, coffee spoons and servers – for years and they're perfect for use on a modern dining table. Juxtaposing is the key.

MAKE IT SPECIAL

Push the boat out by adding to the individual place settings. Photographs are a fun way to direct your guests to their seat, or attach handwritten tags to wine glasses. Bring the outside in by adding a sprig of greenery to each place setting – garden cuttings

such as eucalyptus are perfect for this purpose. Use greenery too for decoration, whether it's a big occasion or just a family meal. You can't beat a bunch of fresh garden foliage in a vase to brighten the table.

CREATE A FOCAL POINT

A drinks bar is an excellent addition to your dining room and super easy to pull together. A tea trolley (or tea wagon) is ideal, as it can be moved about, but any surface would work. Style it up with your favourite drinks, mixers, an ice bucket and a cocktail shaker with a handwritten cocktail menu for your guests to make their choice. Finally, add pretty glassware – seek out Babycham coupes or champagne saucers for the wow factor and the ultimate in hosting prowess.

LIGHT IT UP

Don't forget to get the lighting right. There's nothing worse than a glaring overhead light when you're trying to enjoy your dinner. Use subtle, low-level lighting in the room and then add candles to your main table to add a cosy, welcoming ambience. Nailed it.

Tablescapes for Everyday

It's a true fact that, historically, the only time that we generally make an effort with our dining table decoration is for big holidays, such as Christmas or Thanksgiving. However, as we move toward a more sustainable lifestyle, we are spending more time creating homes that we love, more time at home and more time making the most of connections with our friends and family. Getting together around a table to enjoy a meal and a chat, making memories, is something that has become a regular occurrence in our social calendars.

But taking time to create a beautiful table shouldn't only be for special occasions. As someone whose dining table is generally covered with an abundance of non-dining-related content including, but not limited to, unopened mail, hayfever tablets (my daughter's), football socks and children's homework, there is nothing that I enjoy more than whisking it all away and making it look lovely. Even though I then need to spend the next two hours explaining to my family where I've put everything. Add a tablecloth as a starter for ten – the fabric sections of thrift shops often hold an abundance of lovely floral patterns. You can also work with what you have – white flat sheets are the perfect table size and can be updated with a quick wash through with fabric dye in the colour of your choice. A simple and cost-effective way to add layers to your table.

Greenery is a must when a table isn't in use. In fact, greenery on your table is a must at all times. If you've got a garden, it's the perfect place to pillage for cuttings without spending any money. Eucalyptus,

lilac – any sort of pretty branch that can hold up once cut, really – are ideal to create a display. Pop them in a nice thrifted vase or bottle and you're winning. Think seasonal. Holly and berries during winter are easily foraged and last for ages. Bringing the outside in makes a real difference to your home environment, proven to increase your happiness levels. Create a central display with a tray and add a candle and some small accessories – natural textures such as beach-found shells or pebbles are excellent for this purpose.

Making the most of what you have can make a real difference to your everyday table styling. There may be only two of you for dinner, but it's still nice to make the effort. Your favourite dishes will make even the smallest salad look twice as nice and bring a sense of occasion to a boring Monday evening. Even when we have a family takeaway, I like to light the candles and set the table with napkins and my favourite china and glasses, much to my family's amusement. I can tell you now that you can't beat a burger and fries by candlelight on a vintage platter. These are simple things, but it makes what is a basic meal into something a little bit more special. Bring it every day, not just high days and holidays.

I love planning a pretty table. If we're expecting guests, I've been known to set the table at least two days before. Obsessive, not. No one is allowed to touch it once done and should they remove anything from the table for normal day-to-day living such as plates, condiments, knives or forks, they do so on pain of death. What goes on the table, stays on the table. I ransack my ten-year collection of vintage glassware and china, which generally means every place setting has at least three glasses, and the seated person spends most of their time asking which one to use. I always personalize each place so that my guests know where to sit. I like to have fun with it, often printing a black-and-white photograph of each guest and attaching it to their wine glass or napkin rather than doing more traditional place settings. As a non-traditionalist when it comes to table decor, I tend to use lots of different colours and vintage bits and pieces when building up the look.

We all have busy lives and taking the time to sit, chat and eat together can make a real difference to our wellbeing and happiness. It's easy just to grab something out of the fridge, but spending a moment to set a table and make it special is always worth the effort. Being resourceful with what we have in our homes will help to create the perfect moment.

EVERYDAY TABLE-SETTING CHECKLIST

1. A table centrepiece attracts the eye when the table isn't in use. Anchor the look with a tray or platter.

2. Turn to your garden for greenery – eucalyptus is excellent for adding both beauty and scent, plus foraged branches are very effective.

3. Scour the thrift shops for fabric remnants or vintage sheets for both tablecloths and napkins.

4. Have fun with your accessories – old photographs are a talking point and give your table originality.

5. Finally, make every day a day to celebrate – light the candles and get out the vintage china, even if you're just having beans on toast.

Above: *A photograph of your guest adds a fun personal touch.*
Below: *Small accessories make each place setting unique.*

CASE STUDY

Emilie Fournet's Home

Emilie Fournet is an interior designer who set up her interior design studio, Emilie Fournet Interiors, just over six years ago. Specializing in residential interior design for private clients and architectural partnerships, Emilie was born and raised in France but has been living in London for 20 years. Her beautiful Victorian terraced home is in north London and is typical of the era. Emilie lives with her husband Ben and their two children, Orson (10) and Cosima (6).

I first 'met' Emilie online four years ago, and her dining space with its flowing abundance of plants mixed with vintage pieces and pops of colour immediately sang to me. She describes her style as eclectic and her home designs are based on the context, emotional reaction and connection to objects, colours and styles. Emilie favours particular periods of style history and this is reflected in her surroundings, with art deco, mid-century modern, antiques and more contemporary pieces all playing their part in the overall look.

As most people do, Emilie started furnishing her home with very few funds. Finding herself in a new city, wanting to live in a space that was functional, attractive and fitted her budget, she bought secondhand and vintage furniture. These pieces were picked for their functional purpose, solid quality and were beautiful in their own way. This wasn't new territory for Emilie. She learned to know what to buy and how to judge quality from her mother. As a child in France, she travelled with her family to all the flea markets and antiques stores that surrounded her hometown and she is still a regular visitor. Emilie buys on instinct, but will always seek out pieces that reflect her love of mid-century, art deco or Arts and Crafts styles. Over the years, she has come to love the work and care that has gone into these movements; the devotion and skill of the craftsmen who produced furniture during these periods of design is what keeps Emilie going back to the markets of her childhood.

OPPOSITE: Emilie's plant-adorned dining room opens out onto her garden, creating a space that truly brings the outside in. The vintage chairs have been re-covered in modern botanical fabric that pulls the whole look together.

Why do you furnish your home resourcefully?

I love the sheer quality, timelessness and durability of vintage. Adding pieces from design history can elevate the experience of being in a space. Vintage is never just 'old things' – they reflect history and character. We're actually talking about the result of explosive moments in art and design that revolutionized how we live, even now. I am always pleased to find a space for iconic design in my own home, and for my clients.

Your dining area is beautiful. Which is your favourite piece within this space?

It has to be the dresser. It is a 1940–50s typical 'Mado' French kitchen dresser. My grandmother had one similar and I always wanted one too, so there's a real emotional connection there. I have always loved how the doors and cupboard drawers were curved. I found this one on a selling website, the French version of Gumtree. It cost €20 – not counting the cost of bringing it to the UK, which was achieved by taking it to pieces and putting it in the back of the car at the end of a visit to my parents.

Originally it was a kind of bright yellow colour, which we spent days stripping back. When we moved house, one of the original glass cupboard door was shattered. My mother and I cried when she told me what had happened (true story). It's a shame, but the broken window is now just another part of its history. I can't imagine having my kitchen without this dresser now.

The table and chairs are one of the first things I noticed on your Instagram feed. How did you source them?

I found the chairs when my husband and I lived in our first apartment in London with our newborn son. We had been renting for years, and after finally managing to buy a place, we had little money left for furniture.

They were originally covered in a brown and orange corduroy, which we covered in a floral fabric that suited our extendable dining table at the time. When we moved to the new house, I wanted a round white Tulip table, plus I wanted to fill the kitchen with plants as a way of connecting the new space with the small garden, so we chose this fabric. It's also an outdoor fabric so not only does it look great, it's also really practical as the children constantly wipe their hands on them.

What do plants bring to your space?

They are good for your house generally. They purify the air. They bring peace. They bring the outdoors indoors. They are good for your mental and physical health. They can cost a lot less than an elaborate piece of sculpture, and yet be just as captivating. In the case of my kitchen, the plants go a long way to reconciling the sacrifice of outside space for a good-sized family kitchen. We live as a family in this room, and whenever the weather allows, we open up into our modest outside space. The plants inside are an essential part of that harmony.

OPPOSITE: Emilie brought this kitchen display unit back from France. A glass pane was smashed in transit so she replaced it with wire webbing, which gives the cupboard a unique feel and adds personality.

Where do you shop for something unique?

Everywhere. The key to this is that to find something unique, you should never leave any source untapped. I use all the usual places – eBay, Vinteriors, British Heart Foundation, as well as local vintage suppliers, European websites, flea markets, the street, anywhere!

What are your top three styling tips for a dining space?

1. Good lighting. Make the space where you will eat is inviting, really consider your lighting and how this is going to create different moods for different occasions.

2. Create a focal point where you can always gather. Use flowers in a nice vase, plants in interesting planters, fruits in bowls, anything that makes the space feel welcoming.

3. Make sure it's comfortable. You want people to be drawn in, to feel welcome at your table to eat. Don't put them on bone-hard chairs. Give them somewhere they can sit and enjoy your company. There's nothing worse than an uncomfortable chair.

THIS PAGE above: *Vintage bamboo planters and woven baskets add texture.* **Below:** *Combining different tones of glassware creates a focal point.* ***OPPOSITE:*** *Framing a dish towel is a great way to add art to your space.* ***OVERLEAF:*** *There are lots of textures and layers in Emilie's dining area.*

Have you got any tips for adding vintage to your home?

Research! The history of design is fascinating and easy to access. If you like something you see in a magazine or in a TV show (I am obsessed with TV period set design – those designers are heroic in their efforts to bring style and art into focus on the small screen), then find out more about it. If you have a family heirloom, or just a memory of a piece of furniture, you can try to find out more. You can discover your own connection to period classics. Encourage your interest in design and let yourself see it wherever you go. When buying vintage, you have to be open to the opportunities as they come along. Sometimes you have to buy pieces you don't yet need. And, equally, you have to have the courage to pass on items it is no longer the time for in your life. So listen to your instinct – if you are attracted to a piece, then go for it.

As an interior designer, how do you get the right balance between vintage and modern without making your house an homage to years past?

Choose key pieces and find the right balance – know when to stop. You have to be precise about the use of the furniture you're buying, and the overall aesthetic of your space. We are all made up of hundreds, if not thousands, of experiences and influences. If you stay true to yourself, you can avoid becoming a museum. If you stay disciplined in your need for function, you can avoid living in chaos. You have to think about having just enough, but never too much.

Find Emilie online @emiliefournetinteriors
www.emiliefournetinteriors.com

COOKING AND EATING

Throughout our many years of houses (a quite ridiculous nine moves in 16 years), I have never had a brand new kitchen. And, let me tell you, we've lived in some crackers. More of a Poundland (or dollar store) cracker with a plastic puzzle and a hat that rips upon opening than a Fortnum & Mason gold-embossed, but I've made the most of each one. When my oldest children were tiny, we lived in a 1930s semidetached house in which the standard galley kitchen had been knocked into what would have been the dining space. The previous owners had also added a small conservatory extension, so small that they may actually have built it themselves. Its hollow walls were a haven for rats from the park behind, and they would then access the rest of the house via the gaps in between the floors. Despite the fact that I'm not making the living area sound very appealing, it was actually a great open-plan space and the kitchen was made of solid wood, albeit at least ten years old. I changed the floor, painted the cupboards and the wall, made new blinds and swapped the ceiling lights, which were so dull that you were likely to do yourself a major injury when chopping onions due to lack of glare, replacing them with bright spotlights, which had the dual benefit of saving you from a hospital visit while alerting you to every crumb. I loved it, mostly because I had updated it myself and, as a result, it really, truly reflected my personality.

Research shows that in the UK, we spend at least an hour in the kitchen every day. It's a place to talk, a place to catch up about your day and, most of all, a place to cook and create. Often described as the hub of the home, it can also be a place of carnage unless it's planned and utilized properly. Not to mention that it is one of the most expensive parts of our homes to update. A new kitchen can cost tens of thousands and when we move into a new home, whether rented or purchased, the choice of kitchen is never ours, but that of the previous owners. One of the most popular questions I receive on my blog comes from people who have inherited a room that just doesn't tick any of their boxes. Therein, of course, lies the problem. Kitchens are the same as any other space in your home – if it's not your style, then you won't feel happy.

Style aside, your kitchen space has a big old job to do. Not just a place to cook food or shout at your partner for not emptying the dishwasher, it's a room of often multiple uses. It may be a functional, utilitarian space on paper, but it's regularly multitasking as a dining room or breakfast bar, home bar, work or study space and nearly always as a focal meeting point for social occasions. It's where you make the coffee, eat your breakfast, listen to the news, live your life. As Jona Lewie sang, there's a reason why you'll always find me in the kitchen at parties. Although to be fair, that's probably because it's where the drinks are.

OPPOSITE: A mix of modern and vintage plates in tonal colours creates an interesting focal point across the chimney breast.

Space Planning

As the saying goes, it's not how big it is, it's what you do with it, and this is particularly applicable to the kitchen. Our previous home, an Edwardian semi, had the smallest kitchen that we'd taken on to date. It was a tiny, square space with what would originally have been an outside toilet attached and an elaborately named yet prone-to-mould 'utility room' that included enough space for a fridge, plus a tumble dryer and washing machine piled on top of each other. It wasn't the dream. A door opened on to a large conservatory and Joe and I spent many happy hours planning our perfect open-plan, glass-topped, exposed beamed kitchen that we'd be able to have once these two spaces were knocked into one. Unfortunately, our bank account was unable to cater for these heady expectations, mostly because it had a balance of approximately 56p (70 cents) for 99 per cent of the time due to having three children under seven and only one main income. Combined with my own personal shocking financial history (I'm possibly the only person ever to have had a court action taken out against them for an outstanding balance of £26 ($34) from The Book Club, obtained due to pure laziness), these extension dreams were but a pie in the sky. But still, I loved that kitchen and made it my own.

There is no such thing as the 'one size fits all' kitchen. Every person, every family is different and has different needs. Adapting what you inherit to suit those needs can seem like a daunting task, nay, impossible. The kitchen is part of the bones of your house. When you move into a new home, you're most often stuck with it for at least a year or two. You can't lift up and swap around those units or worktop, can't rearrange the layout. The previous resident of your home may have had a penchant for country chic – basket drawers, roman blinds, wooden worktop. All very nice. But if you yearn for a minimal loft-style white gloss units with soft-close drawers and a floor-to-ceiling wine fridge, then it's not going to float your boat. Although let's face it, a floor-to-ceiling wine fridge would have me sailing off into the distance. And even if you are lucky enough to have the budget for a brand spanking new kitchen, how do you ensure that you're not riding on a trend and that you'll still love your choices in a few years' time? It's a conundrum, for sure.

Let's start with lack of space, which is an all too often complaint. How do you streamline your kitchen to make sure you're making the most of what you have? Getting the storage situation right is key. The first step is to clear out the kitchen. Work out exactly what you need to have in the space. How often do you use the blender? Or the fondue set that you won in a raffle back in 2007? Rarely, but I'll bet it takes up at least half a cupboard. Donate, sell or box up and store in the garage or shed. Chuck out all the chipped plates and consolidate what remains – do you need a stack of 25 in your kitchen when there are only four of you? Box up 15 and store them away. The same applies to china, mugs (the last time I cleared out my kitchen I donated a grand total of 26) and that huge casserole dish that you only use at Christmas or Thanksgiving. Be ruthless. If you have a utility room, make the most of it – allocate a cupboard for items that are not so regularly used and another for cans and dried food.

Tackle the drawer of Tupperware – if you've lost the lid, send it off to recycling. And why do you still have plastic cups and bowls when your children are about to take their final exams? Donate or recycle to someone who has the glorious years of toddler feeding ahead of them. Empty out the food cupboard, including the can of carrots dating from 1996 and date-check your herbs and spices (I always fall down on this one, although I'm unconvinced that a bit of out-of-date cumin can cause any harmful effects). Be brutal. It'll be worth it when you're able to open a drawer without swearing due to it being stuck from overfilling. Allocate different cupboards to different products and invest in space-saving containers for your baking ingredients and condiments so that you can bring them out easily when required, instead of having to spend half an hour locating them in seven different areas of the room.

You've cleared the decks, you're feeling organized, but the kitchen still feels cramped. The second thing to consider is removing the wall units and replacing them with open shelves. I have done this in every single home we have had. There are two good reasons for this. Firstly, it completely opens up the space. I've had homes with galley kitchens that feel dark and overcrowded; removing the units brings in the light and makes the whole room feel much more spacious. Secondly, it enables you to make your kitchen a room that reflects you, not a kitchen showroom, by enabling you to display your most beautiful pieces and add personality.

In summary, think of this as your guide: hide the less pretty, the boring stuff, in well-planned spaces and bring out the beauty that will make the room your own. Adding basketware, cookbooks and attractive

stacked plates and bowls will draw the eye, creating a focal point in your kitchen while providing functional storage – the perfect way to multitask what you have.

THIS PAGE: Displaying your favourite plates and dishes is both practical and pretty. OVERLEAF: The white worktop, walls and pale lilac cupboards of my kitchen provide a neutral base for adding colour and art to the space.

Creating a Style

Deciding how to decorate your kitchen space can be no easy task. We are accosted at every turn by magazines, social media and retailers instructing us in the latest trend, the coolest look, the most current paint colour. One day it's minimal, the next maximal; dark and moody, then light and natural. Oh, the pressure. So which to go for? The answer is simple: none of them. The only look to go for is the one that makes you happy and suits your own personal style. Move away from the trends, people; there's nothing to see here.

So where to start? The same place as you'd start planning all other rooms and that's an inspiration board. Pinterest as if your life depended on it, cut pictures from magazines, scour social media for ideas. Save your favourite looks, everything from lighting through to doorknobs. Save the pictures that you come back to again and again. Save the styles that sing to you, that you are irrevocably drawn to. Add items that are on your wish list, such as nice china or statement cupboard handles. Before long, you'll find a theme, and from there you can start to make the changes.

If you have a budget, then invest in the hard-core elements. Flooring, worktops, taps and sinks would be top of my hit list in the event of any excess cash. All other elements of the room can be easily changed but the bones of your kitchen are the long-haul basis of your workspace. Try to think long term and avoid being influenced by what's currently 'in'. You may be smitten by a statement colour tap or basin, but if you decide to paint your cupboards, will it still blend in quite as nicely? The answer is most probably not. By keeping these investments classic and timeless, you'll be able to update the look of your space at minimum cost as your style evolves.

Use the sell-to-buy method. If you've removed wall cupboards or swapped the cupboard handles, stick them on a local selling site and add to your kitchen fund. Look at what you have and be resourceful – it's not always necessary to invest in the new when the old simply needs a bit of love and attention. Making the most of what you already have is a sustainable way to update your home and there are plenty of ways to do this.

Consider it not just as a functional space, but as a room in itself. Paint is a healer when it comes to tending to an unloved room. The biggest transformation that you can make in the kitchen is to paint the cupboards. I know, I know. People veer away from this, worried that they will mess it up, that it will chip. But let's face it, if your kitchen cupboards are making your heart sink every time you walk into the room, then any change is a good one. A fresh coat of paint and a change of cupboard handles is a game changer. If the doors are past painting, consider working with a local carpenter to change them completely using moisture-resistant wood. Paint the window frames or doors – I have done this in my kitchen with black paint and it's completely changed the look of the space when combined with crisp white walls. Tile paint is another bonus product that is often overlooked.

OPPOSITE: Emilie Fournet's simple white kitchen is lifted by the graphic tiles, artwork and vintage accessories.

THIS PAGE: Textured brass handles add interest to the cupboard doors. OPPOSITE above: An oak worktop offcut creates a run of shelving for display. Below: A statement tap and cast-iron sink bring the luxe factor to a simple kitchen.

Bring in accessories just as you would in any other space. No kitchen is complete without the personal touches. Add art to your walls or prop it on your kitchen shelves for layered height and shop your home for pieces that will blend with your scheme. There are no boundaries – my previous kitchen featured a beaded palm tree room divider, an entire wall of religious iconic images collected from holidays and a vintage plate wall. Plants are an essential to bring the outside in, and it's much easier to remember to water when they're placed in a room with a sink.

As a woman who has had many kitchens in many houses but has never once installed her own, these changes have taken me through many years of difficult spaces. It's easy to look at an unsatisfactory kitchen and think it's an insurmountable problem, but it doesn't take much money to really make a difference and to create a room that suits you and your personality. Every room in your house should make your heart sing, and the kitchen is no exception. Think sell, donate, reuse and repurpose and you'll soon have a room that will tick the box.

Storage and Display

EVALUATE WHAT YOU HAVE

Look at what you've got. Do you need to add storage? Assess your room and plan where it could go. If you have wall space, add shelving. If you have wall cupboards, are they functional? A light-up display cabinet may look lovely but it's not the greatest use of space. Consider removing them and replacing with open shelving. If you have utility space, look at what you have and plan the best way it can be used.

REASSESS WHAT YOU NEED

Assess the china and cutlery required in your kitchen based on how many are living in your home. The same applies to glassware and mugs – it's easy

to build up a huge collection of drinking vessels of which you only ever use two favourites. Big serving dishes and platters are great for parties but don't need to take up space in an everyday cupboard. Store the excess elsewhere to be accessed when needed.

DONATE, RECYCLE OR REPURPOSE

Look at the kitchen items that you are not using on a regular basis. Do you love them? If you do, keep them and store. If you don't, donate, recycle or repurpose. My friends and I often WhatsApp for homeware swaps – you may have never used the George Foreman griddle that you got from your mother-in-law five years ago, but it might be on their wish list.

INVEST IN STORAGE

It's worth investing in storage options for items like herbs, spices, dried food (rice, pasta) and baking goods. Decant into containers pretty enough to use on your shelves and use chalk labels so that you don't forget what's in them. Wooden wine boxes not only add texture but are also excellent storage solutions.

GROUP TOGETHER

Allocate each storage area with a purpose to avoid carnage, whether it be oils and condiments, cereals, canned food or pet food. Giving a cupboard or shelf a specific function means it's less likely to get out of control. If you have space, put up a hanging rail for your pans and utensils to free up other areas.

CREATE FOCAL POINTS

Make practical areas interesting by creating focal points – turn your coffee maker space into barista heaven by adding cool coffee pod storage and your favourite, aesthetically pleasing cups. Style it up with a plant and a tray to store all the essentials. And don't forget a tin full of biscotti for the authentic coffee shop feel.

MAKE IT PRACTICAL

Use every inch of space that you have. That empty wall above the radiator? The back of the kitchen or pantry door? Paint it in blackboard paint and use it as a place for reminders and events. But don't stop there – scour Pinterest for blackboard art and get creative with the chalk by adding word art, plant drawings, whatever you feel like. Don't be wary of giving it a go – it's great fun.

THINK ABOUT ART

Treat your kitchen as you would any other room in your home and add art to the walls. Again, if you love it, there's no reason why you can't display it (did I mention I once had a full wall of iconic religious images that I'd collected on holiday?). Use prints on your shelves, propping them up as a backdrop to your favourite china and glassware. Vintage oils picked up in thrift shops are a brilliant juxtaposition to more modern pieces and draw the eye – use alongside modern typography for impact.

CURATE A COLLECTION

I've covered the chimney breast above the stove in our home with plates, vintage and modern, which I've collected over the years. Individually, they look a little plain – together, they're a cohesive collection. Theme your shelves and kitchen displays in colour tones for visual effect. Stack your plates and bowls so that they become focal points in themselves. All white is forever stylish or mix several tones of the same colour to add interest to your space. Combine with glassware, wicker or wood to mix up the texture.

BRING THE OUTSIDE IN

Finally, don't forget to add plants. Open shelves are crying out for trailing or hanging plants, and kitchens are a great place to keep them, especially because of their proximity to the sink, which means you're less likely to forget to water them. Pillage your garden (or someone else's garden, preferably someone you know) for bunches of greenery that you can whack in a big vase for your kitchen table centrepiece. Green is the colour of life and energy, perfect for a busy kitchen environment.

*OPPOSITE: Combining kitchen accessories in similar earthy tones is very effective. **THIS PAGE:** Strengthened picture ledges are perfect for displaying bottles that are too pretty to hide away.*

Multipurposing

When we moved into our house here in York, the kitchen was the very first room that I updated. I have to say that this wasn't a decision that made me very popular with my husband, Joe. The house had been renovated by a property developer, who had installed a spanking new, gleaming country chic beauty, complete with granite worktop and light-up glass wall cupboards. For many, this kitchen would have been the dream. As mentioned previously, we have never before had a new kitchen – we* (*read me) had spent many hours planning our dream space without the cash to back up our plans. This cream-coloured, pillared-unit stunner was Joe's dream. From his perspective, all that was missing were the white leather pump-action comfort padded island bar stools. This is a man, I might add, who would have inset spotlights in every room in the house if he were given the chance. Unfortunately, our personal kitchen dream goals were continents apart and, as the person who spent the most time in the space, I decided that changes had to be made. The kitchen wasn't working for us as a family – it needed to be more flexible, more of a family space than a glossy showroom. So I pushed for change. And won. Obviously (I always win). I recycled, repurposed and reallocated to create a room that sang with my own personality and was multifunctional for the way that we lived as a family.

In these days of resourceful living, every single inch of our homes has to work hard. Most of us don't have the luxury of excess space, so being clever with how we use the spaces we do have is an essential. The kitchen is the most popular room in the house and, as such, often has several uses, especially for families or multiple occupants. Breakfast bars and tables often act as the focus of the room and are regularly used for either working from home or, in the case of the kids, homework. In my own home, it's painful enough to get my children to sit down and do it, so I try to make it as easy as possible by having a mini IKEA trolley in the corner complete with everything required for the task. This seems quite simple, but it makes a huge difference when you're clearing away at the end of the day. Just having a place to drop bags and lunchboxes makes life much simpler and less stressful than harassing the kids to move them from the hallway so that you don't fall over them.

You can make your kitchen work for you by allocating spaces for practical purpose. Utilizing a corner of your kitchen for a coffee space is an excellent way to create a focal point and add some personality. Position your coffee maker and group your favourite cups – add a small shelf above and store your coffee and sugar in pretty containers, adding a tumbler of spoons for easy access. Or make your own home bar – a wine rack (wall- or worktop-mounted) will add contrast alongside a collection of vintage crystal glassware and an ice bucket. Add a tray for mixers and a bowl filled with limes and lemons and you'll have everything to hand for that end-of-the-day cocktail.

OPPOSITE: A corner of the family room has been utilized as a home bar space. The bar itself is a basic wooden structure that has been tiled and painted to create more of a feature. Wicker bar stools add contrasting texture.

Utility rooms are often overlooked when it comes to use of space. When we first moved into our home, ours housed the laundry machines plus a haggard selection of wall and base units. It was a dumping ground for pretty much everything (mostly football kits and empty plastic bags), a windowless room with no natural light and absolutely nothing going for it. The cupboards were full of all the things that I couldn't find a home for and never looked at. After working out what I actually used, I redistributed, donated or recycled the contents and whipped the wall units off, replacing them with three levels of scaffold shelves. Redecoration of the base units, new handles and a feature wallpaper transformed the space from a dark room of doom into a brighter space that was far more conducive to use. I added a pull-down dryer rail and a row of hooks, then allocated one of the cupboards to store tins, grains and flours. I invested in storage for pet food, washing powders, herbs and spices and stocked the shelves full of my baking and serving equipment, which had always previously overloaded the cupboards. The utility room was now multitasked as a pantry.

*OPPOSITE: The Poodle & Blonde wallpaper behind the pale pink scaffold shelving is a feature in itself. **THIS PAGE**: Make the most of every inch of storage space by adding wooden hooks, bought from eBay.*

KITCHEN REVAMP
CHECKLIST

1. ASSESS THE STORAGE

Work out exactly what you need. Count up your china and mugs and discard any that are chipped or broken, then, putting aside enough for daily use, box up the rest for when you have guests. Look at your appliances. If you don't use something at least once a week, store it away. That includes, but isn't limited to, fondue sets, food processors, sandwich makers and deep fat fryers, all of which are space hogs.

2. UPDATE THE CUPBOARDS

Removing the wall cupboards and replacing with open shelving expands the space. Smaller kitchens can often feel dark and overcrowded; making this change brings in the light. Source a local carpenter to make you new solid shelves or wooden fronts to measure – an investment, but a good one. Be clever – whack the cupboards on eBay and swap the handles on your base units for a new look.

3. GET OUT THE PAINTBRUSH

The biggest transformation you can make in your kitchen is to paint, whether we're talking kitchen walls or cupboards. It seems like a challenge but it's one worth taking on – a change of cupboard colour can completely update the look of your space. Be brave and try it yourself, but make sure you prime first!

4. UPDATE THE TILES

If you don't like the tiles in your kitchen, paint them. My sister painted an entire floor-to-ceiling red kitchen in white tile paint and no one was any the wiser. You can also paint the floor if it doesn't suit your style – check with your local store as to which paint to use.

5. SWITCH THE LIGHTING

It's oh so easy just to stick spotlights in the kitchen ceiling and be done with it. But where is the ambience? They certainly don't fit with my 'the kitchen should be treated like any other room' ethos one bit. Add to the spots with a statement ceiling light over a breakfast bar or table for impact.

6. ACCESSORIZE

Finish off your newly updated kitchen with a styling fest. Use your shelves to display your favourite china and cookery books and add plenty of plants. Prop your favourite art on the shelves and pop it on the walls to bring the room together. Shop your home for pieces that will add your personality to the space and don't hold back. I have a plate wall above the oven to which I regularly add favourite new finds.

7. INVEST IN THE BEST

And, finally, if you DO have a budget, then invest in the hard-core elements that aren't going anywhere, such as flooring, worktops and taps. These are the bones of your home and need to last. Think carefully about your choices and avoid trend-based decisions, bearing in mind that your style can evolve and the trend that you love now you may well regret in a few years' time.

MENU

STARTERS
CHOPPED SOUP
HORSE EGG SALAD
MOMENT
WASP OMELETTE
GHOSTS

DESSERTS
FOAM
SOGGY BUNS
CAKEY PONY
RAISINS
MEETING

MAINS
CHUBBY CHICKEN
SMUG FLAN
LEFT OVERS
8 PEAS

COCKTAILS
GUILTY PHONECALL
ABOUT THE HOUSE
WHENEVER
ADVERT FOR A CAR
EASY MIND
ONE WHOLE

(champignon de couche)   LES CHAMPIGNONS
Chapeau

Lamelles produisant
les spores
Spores tombant
des lamelles

Anneau

Fruits ou
champignons

Mousseron

Coulemelle

Pied
Très jeune fruit

Morilles

La plante ou thalle est né d'une spore

Truffe

Le champignon n'est que le fruit d'une plante, ou thalle

Quelques champignons comestibles

Les champignons sont des plantes parasites, sans racines, sans tiges, sans feuilles et sans chlorophylle

ATTENTION AUX CHAMPIGNONS VENENEUX!

Bolet comestible
ou Cèpe de Bordeaux

Bolet tête de nègre

Bolet amer (veneneux)

Bolet Satan (veneneux)

Girolle ou Chanterelle

Fausse girolle (veneneux)

Lactaire tache

Lactaire veneneux

Russule Palumet

Russule de Quelet (veneneux)

Clavaire jaune

Clavaire dorée (veneneux)

CASE STUDY

Lisa's Kitchen

When we moved into our home in May 2015, the entire house had been completely renovated by a property developer. The house was, effectively, a blank canvas; the kitchen and the bathrooms were all brand new and there was nothing structural to be done whatsoever. For me, it was basically a dream; my ideas for each room overflowed and thus my addiction to documenting what I did on Instagram was born.

Anyway, the kitchen was cream. Literally, all cream. The walls, the cupboards, the floor. An abundance of cream, more cream than a dairy farm, in fact. The kitchen had wall units with glass fronts and internal lights to display my grubby glassware to all. There was an island bar in the centre (Joe was in his element; he'd always had a dream of sitting at an island bar with a MacBook and a coffee, like some life insurance ad). However, I really didn't like it very much. I had an aversion to wall units – I've always been a fan of open shelving – and the colour of the cupboards and matching twisted brass handles did nothing for me. The problem was that it was all brand new. Not only was there no justification to replace it, but I didn't have the budget to do so even if I could convince myself otherwise. Which, it has to be said, I couldn't.

So, in the summer of 2016, I decided to update it. Joe and I removed the wall units and replaced them with oak shelves which I had custom-made by a local carpenter. I added a central light, painted the unit doors navy blue, changed the cupboard handles and bought a huge vintage Persian rug for £120 ($157) from eBay, which transformed the space. I was MUCH happier with it. However – rather predictably – two and a half years later, I decided it was time for a change.

OPPOSITE: I kept the kitchen carcasses, as I was happy with the layout, and swapped the cupboard doors for plywood. I painted them to match my favourite nail colour (Essie Lilacism) but I can always easily update them if I want to change the look again.

I'd seen a kitchen on Pinterest that had a combination of textures that really made me happy. Ply doors, wooden floor, farmhouse table, neutral decor. The whole effect was light and bright but also sustainable and bursting with natural materials. I wanted this look for my own kitchen so I investigated how I could incorporate these components but also recycle and donate what I no longer needed without resorting to landfill. Just a small task, then. So what did I do? First off, I removed the ornate cupboards surrounding the fridge which I'd always disliked. They came off easily and created an entire cupboard width of space which meant, most importantly, that the worksurface could be extended, adding extra space. I uploaded the cupboards to Freecycle and they were collected within a day to be used in someone else's project.

As mentioned above, I was kind of over navy kitchens. However, despite looking a bit battered, the paintwork had held up well. But I needed a change. I still loved the layout of my kitchen and I didn't want to replace the carcasses – they were in perfectly good order and totally acceptable to be reused. The answer? Replace the doors only. I found a UK-based company that specialized in sustainable plywood fronts made to your specification and I really liked the idea of using a natural material that would last. I posted the old doors on Freecycle and they were collected within a day by a couple who had bought a renovation project.

The dark cupboards were too dark, I had stopped feeling the love for the navy and, indeed, the brown worktop, which had never really gelled with the rest of the room. I'd already removed the island bar and replaced it with a table and chairs, which was far more practical. I'd gone off the central brown beaded chandelier – it felt fussy and, again, too dark for the room. Altogether, it was looking a little bit shabby. I needed to make some changes, but the kitchen was only four years old. I was happy with the layout; it would have been sacrilege, quite frankly, to rip out perfectly good cupboards and replace them with new. But it didn't feel 'right' to me. Mornings in our house are frantic with kids rushing for the school bus and I wanted to transform it into a calm and neutral space, but also to make it cosy and welcoming.

The one item I wished I'd been able to change in the kitchen when I revamped the space the first time was the worktop. A dark brown, it was excellent quality but the colour didn't fit with the scheme one bit. I replaced it with a new marble worktop I knew would look amazing with the plywood fronts and the old worktop went to a builder friend who repurposed them in a student house. The perfect circle of worktop life.

Now to the walls. White was the only way to go; a neutral background, enabling me to change other elements of the kitchen in future should I wish to do so (from experience, likely). But I took it a step further, painting the ceiling in gloss paint. This is an excellent top tip – the gloss enables the light to bounce off the work surface and around the room, making the space significantly lighter, a trick that works particularly well in smaller spaces. I also painted the window frames – it's a dual-aspect room – and the door in black, which contrasted beautifully with the walls and the cupboards. Paint is a truly brilliant way to update a room at minimum cost.

OPPOSITE: Approach your kitchen shelving in the same way as you approach your living shelving – style them up. THIS PAGE: Always in the kitchen at parties – it's simple to create a bar area for guests.

The key factor for me in creating my dream kitchen was light. Lots of it. But also light that could be dimmed for a romantic meal for two (an annual experience, but no less important). I updated the recessed ceiling spotlights to LED and added classic task lighting above the shelving. These were an investment, but a timeless one that added significantly to the space. I needed a central light and I wanted to find something that was clean-lined and simple, in sympathy with the rest of the kitchen style. I trawled eBay for a Louis Poulsen vintage light. Again, I figured it was a good investment and the style is a design classic that will never date. It's on a dimmer switch and perfectly positioned above the table to change the ambience of the space when needed.

We had bought our house complete with a workbench in the garage, which I hadn't really examined closely. It was at least a couple of hundred years old, stained with varnish and huge dollops of paint and wasn't particularly attractive. Because the bench was so deep, I asked a carpenter to cut the legs down to make it suitable for a dining table. I used an orbital sander to remove the years of staining. One thing that I hadn't really taken into account when I started on the project was the fact it needed three people minimum to lift it. Basically, it's four logs strapped together and weighs a ton. At least. Anyway, after a minor* (*read major) disaster, when Joe and I managed to drop the table and it split in half (resolved with several very large brackets), it eventually made it into the kitchen where I used clear Danish wood oil and painted the legs in black chalk paint to finish it off. It's one of my favourite pieces in my home and makes me really happy. Who knows who has sat at the table before us? The history of the table adds to the appeal.

I hung some favourite pieces of art on the walls and created a focal point by using vintage and modern plates on the chimney breast that I'd collected over the years from thrift shops and small stores. I was ruthless in my thinning down of china, donating and recycling all the old mugs, bowls and plates that no longer worked for me. I restyled the shelves using my favourite pieces, adding accessories and propping art behind as a feature. I selected my most used cookery books and stacked them on the shelves so that they were easily accessible, and used decorative plant pots to store utensils alongside the hob (or cooktop). Finally, I used dhurrie-style rugs on the floor, which could be easily lifted and shaken to keep the space sparkling clean. Not that anywhere in my home is often sparkling clean – I can but try.

I'm really happy with the end result. It feels so much lighter, and the gloss ceiling and white worktops have made a huge difference to the space. The revamped table is bigger than the old one and doubles up as a work space when cooking, which was an unexpected bonus. Removing the excess cupboards has also made a difference and it's a room that the family now linger in for longer than they used to. Repurposing what I already had, recycling what I no longer needed and investing in key pieces that will last the course has created a kitchen that truly does work and, most of all, reflects my own personality.

OPPOSITE: Plants are a kitchen essential and can be trained to trail across the space by using small picture nails.

SLEEPING AND BATHING

In an ideal world, your bedrooms and bathroom should be an oasis of calm; a place to relax, to forget about the stresses of daily life and take moments for yourself to boost your batteries. Our bedrooms are our sanctuaries. Unless, of course, you have young children. For almost two decades, our bedroom has been merely an overnight stop – a very untidy one – en route to the final bastion of my overall decorating plans. It's always been last on the list, given no attention and with no resemblance to any magazine or Pinterest image that I've ever seen. For many years, it seemed as if those pre-kids days of breakfast in bed, long scented baths and sleeping in past 6am were but an urban myth. I once considered launching an Instagram hashtag entitled #foodifindinmybedroom after the empty Pringles tubes and Oreo wrappers from my children's extended baths in our en suite followed by lounging on our bed watching YouTube threatened to push me over the edge.

When we moved into our home, it was a revelation. Not only was the master bedroom a good size but it had what was, for me, the ultimate in home organization – a dressing room. This was extremely lucky. Our previous house, which we had rented for a year, was much smaller and when we moved in, I decided to take my own advice of not owning any furniture that I didn't actually like. Unfortunately, what this meant was that I recklessly sold ALL of our wardrobes on eBay with the result that we lived with our clothes in plastic boxes under our bed for 12 months. This situation was exacerbated by the fact that I am a woman who does not iron. I wash, I tumble-dry, I fold, I leave in a pile in the utility room. Until the situation gets so bad that no one has

OPPOSITE: The bed is the main feature in the Barn Annex bedroom and really makes an impact. **THIS PAGE:** *Simple plywood shelves in the shower room work well for storage and display.*

In my bedroom, I've combined traditional styling with modern statement art for juxtaposition. The wall lights are a space-saving option, freeing up the bedside for essentials.

I'm not sitting here doing nothing. I'm waiting for the end of the world to happen.

any underwear in their rooms. Combine my poor housekeeping skills with the no-wardrobe situation due to my impulsive flogging, and you can well imagine that the plastic boxes were the cause of very many arguments.

Our bedrooms and bathrooms need to work hard for us. As well as being utilized as functional yet aesthetically pleasing storage, they should provide a space of comfortable quiet when winding down at the end of the day. Making the most of our spaces while trying not to overload them with non-essentials is key. Good wardrobe and drawer storage for your clothes and accessories – fitted or freestanding – is imperative. This equally applies to the bathroom – there's nothing worse than discarded toothbrushes and half-squished tubes cluttering up the work surface. Tidy space, tidy mind and all that.

If you're planning a new bathroom, plan well. These are not cheap places to furnish and what you choose now, you'll need to love for a while. Tiles, floors, hardware and sanitaryware are the bones of your home and need to be considered at length. Try not to be influenced by fleeting trends – take a look at the rest of your home when working the core style of the room. Think flexibly. By going for a neutral base, you'll be able to update with accessories as and when you feel like switching it up. The heavily patterned tiles that are all over town may have you rushing to include them in your design, but once they're down, they're down and they're down for a while. Create a moodboard, bringing together all the elements that you want to include to make sure that you're totally happy with how it all blends before you start the process.

In your bedroom, as with all other rooms in your home, multitasking and making the most of what you have already is the key to success. Vintage glass bowls and cups are ideal for storing brushes and cosmetics on your dressing table, large basketware is perfect for towels, or add colour to the room by bringing in layered rugs and cushions. Think about how you are going to use the space – you may need to incorporate a work area or you might have enough room to include a seat and reading corner. Good focused lighting is an essential if you're a bedtime reader, plus plenty of space at the side of the bed for your books and magazines. Think about the textiles – curtains, blinds and bedding. There is much to consider, but it's well worth the time it takes to plan it properly.

THIS PAGE: Typographical art adds impact above a maple wood chest of drawers. OPPOSITE: The dressing-table space in my daughter Ella's bedroom makes the most of every inch and reflects her personality, with photographs of friends, postcards and a never-ending supply of beauty products.

Bedroom moodboard

Feature lighting
When choosing a central light, it needs to look just as good turned off as it does on. This chandelier with its brass interior adds another layer to the room.

Calming greenery
The plant by the bedside brings the outside in.

Natural textures
Incorporating texture was an important part of planning this room. Sisal flooring and the woven cane headboard provide a natural element, and maple wood side tables keep the scheme neutral.

TACTILE FEATURES

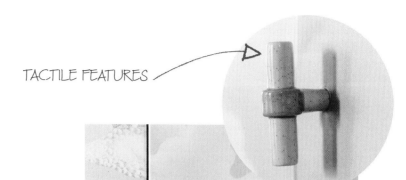

Cosy finishes
The soft velvet curtains work well with the flooring and are super tactile.

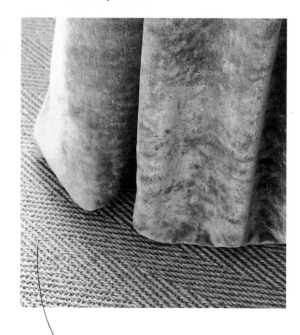

SISAL FLOORING

DIY luxe
A statement wallpaper on the IKEA wardrobe doors means that the dressing-room space becomes a real feature and a room in itself. The ceramic handles from Anthropologie (bought cheaply in the sale) add the luxe factor to what is a simple DIY update.

Your bedroom should be an oasis, a space in which to relax and unwind, filled with things that bring you happiness and reflect your own personal style.

Furniture

When you're planning your home, one of the main objectives is that it reflects your own personal style. Choosing items purposefully with care and love is what will make your home your own – you want to walk through the front door and feel your body relax and your heart lift. Having things around us that feel personal to us is the route to happiness. Your bedroom has a lot of responsibility, not least because we spend a whopping 33 years of our life sleeping. What we surround ourselves with in our own personal sanctuaries will not only lift us up but will also ensure we are relaxed and ready for a good night's sleep.

Adding vintage items is always a good start. My favourite purchase in my bedroom is my dressing table. Picked up for a song at my local Community Furniture Warehouse, it's an original G Plan E Gomme piece with beautiful dovetailed joints and deep drawers. It dates back to the 1950s and comes complete with a huge oval mirror and a large glass worktop. It's a solid piece of furniture and is just as hard-wearing today as it was 70 years ago. Everyone needs a dressing table. Not only do they create a focal point in your bedroom space but they also provide plenty of storage, the perfect hideaway for those items that don't need to be on show. Like sideboards, their popularity dwindled back in the 1980s with the advent of fitted furniture, but they're excellent pieces of furniture and are now back with a vengeance.

The classic bedroom setup of matching side tables, dresser, drawers and wardrobes is long gone. We're holding on to our furniture for longer, making more purposeful choices by sourcing carefully and, as a result, it is now far more eclectic in style. It's a great opportunity for my favourite activity, multitasking. Bedside tables are an excellent example of how you can utilize what you already have in a different way. A wooden chair, for example, has plenty of space for a lamp and book. Blanket boxes are perfect for next to the bedside and provide a larger surface area, especially if you're prone to overloading with magazines, copious facial oils and water glasses, as I am. A recycled wooden tea chest not only adds texture to the room but can be reused in multiple settings. It's the perfect size for your bedside essentials while still adding a sense of history – who knows where the tea chest has been and who it's been used by? It's this type of interesting piece that makes your space special.

A long bench at the end of the bed is practical and also provides a good opportunity to add a thrifted find. Old school benches are the perfect size and ideal for this purpose and, again, they can be used in a variety of ways around your home. Seeking out this type of practical piece is the way to go – the more you can multitask an item of furniture, the more sustainable it is, as you are likely to keep it much longer.

OPPOSITE: Scored for £45 ($58) at my local Community Furniture Store, this vintage dressing table has plenty of storage. The curved edges and craftsmanship make the piece stand out, despite the fact that it is over 70 years old.

OPPOSITE: *This old IKEA chair has been re-covered in teddy bear fabric for added texture.*
THIS PAGE: *A wooden bench provides an extra surface in a small space.*

Making It Work over Time

THIS PAGE: The colour-pop tiles work well with natural textures. OPPOSITE: Adapted wall-hung kitchen cupboards make an excellent vanity base.

When I was planning my family bathroom, I was wholly and utterly convinced by large patterned tiles. Absolutely, one hundred per cent committed to the idea. I'd seen them everywhere, a really popular trend. I created a moodboard to lay out how the room would work so that I could get a good idea of how the finished space would look. However, the gloriously patterned tiles just didn't work. I tried. I did my best. But I couldn't make the moodboard gel and I knew that, ultimately, I'd go off them, much as that infuriated me. I cast aside my dreams of patterned joyousness and went for white, a choice that aligned with my core style.

When you're updating your bathroom, plan with intention and plan well. Look at the space you have – it matters not whether it is big or small, the key elements for consideration are always the same. First of all, assess the space. Work out what you really need – we spend a significant amount of time in these rooms so keep them as spacious as you can. It's tempting to whack a double basin unit in, but is it a practical choice? Measure the space then draw it out on paper so you can work out your perfect design. Next, consider storage. If you're anything like me, you'll have plenty of bathroom products (can you ever have too many?), but keeping them in sensible storage creates cleaner lines. Inset shower shelves can be built into the plan to house toiletries, and shelving can be incorporated into the smallest of spaces. Don't forget towel storage – towel-rail radiators are an excellent practical choice.

Finally, keep it simple. Bathrooms are part of the bones of a home and need to work hard. Your style will evolve so it's important to go for classic, good-quality bathroom furniture that will create a long-lasting base.

Bathroom moodboard

Biophilia
Plants are an essential bathroom addition, adding colour and texture to what is often a small space. If you're lacking in light, go for faux – there are plenty of good-quality options out there.

WICKER MAKES GREAT NEUTRAL STORAGE

Lighting choices
Spotlights are a bathroom essential but double up with more decorative wall lighting for a more subtle glow so that you can change the ambience.

Classic shapes
Pick tiles that will last the course trend-wise and will work with wall colour changes if you fancy an update.

ACRYLIC FRAMING

Decorative additions

Add accessories to your space in the same way as you would to any other room in your home by incorporating tonal glassware and ceramics. Bring in art by framing postcards in acrylic sleeves that protect against steam and heat.

Stylish features

A bathroom mirror doesn't have to be boring – use it as an opportunity to add texture to your room.

Tonal storage

Basketware gives a natural feel to the space while being an excellent storage option.

Creative flooring

Flooring forms part of the bones of your home, so avoid the trends and go for a classic pattern or shape that will work with changes to the space.

WORKING

Working from home is fast becoming the new normal. Recent events have meant that many of us have adjusted an area of our home space to become office space, albeit temporarily, and we've had to get resourceful in our methods to adapt. My own home office is a small room that has become what can only be described as a dumping ground for children's school work, retail shopping bills (immediately whisked away from the main thoroughfare of my home and opened on a need-to-know basis) and a lot of cardboard boxes with contents ranging from fabric samples to picture-hanging nails and a hammer. The room generally looks as if it's been burgled but for me, as a full-time 'work from homer', the space is the centre of my day and it's where I feel comfortable doing my job.

Over the years we have lived here, this space has changed considerably as my working life has evolved but it's always retained the very same elements that flow throughout my home. Vintage furniture mixes with modern IKEA storage; one wall is completely dedicated to a corkboard display and I have picture ledges where I display favourite interiors books and trailing plants. Although I recently invested in a large desk, for many years I worked from a vintage smoked glass Pieff dining table that I picked up on eBay for £50 ($65). If you have the space, a small dining table is perfect for this purpose. Larger than the standard desk, it's a practical yet economical option – secondhand auction sites are full of tables that are surplus to requirements. Teamed with a modern chair, it's a far more interesting way to decorate your working space. You can also repurpose original mid-century consoles or even dressing tables for your working use, both of which will do an excellent job. Shop your home to see if you have anything hanging around that can be multitasked for this purpose.

THIS PAGE: Combined with a vintage sign, picture-ledge storage above the desk enables me to display my favourite books. OPPOSITE: If you have room, facing the desk outward creates a far more welcoming and appealing space.

for when you need it. Look at spaces that don't specifically have a use. When I renovated the garage barn, I utilized the wide hallway that would otherwise have struggled for purpose.

Another option is to take it outside. If you're lucky enough to have a garden, there are plenty of options on the market if you're considering a small summerhouse or room. These are an investment, but a good one if you're looking to add value to your home or are likely to be working there for any significant period of time. They're also perfect for multiuse – by day, it's a working room but, by night, the doors can be opened up to transform it into a social space for cocktails and canapés. Add a sofa bed and you've got a spare room for when friends and family visit.

Creating the perfect working environment is essential for our productivity and there's plenty that we can do to make these spaces, whether large or small, work for us. As with any other room in our home, making it individual and personal while still practical is the key, and utilizing what we already have in our repertoire is the first step. Be creative with your storage so that you don't fall down the hole of paper carnage (my own regular haunt). Shop your home for items that can be multipurposed and surround yourself with happy memories to encourage positivity and, in my case, remind you to concentrate on the job in hand rather than randomly scrolling through your phone for hours. If there were an award for procrastination in the workplace, I would most definitely be a winner.

If you don't have a specific room in which to work and often end up sitting uncomfortably at the kitchen table, there are plenty of other options. Under-stair space is often overlooked and more often used as an area for ditching coats and shoes. You'll find that once the cupboard walls are removed, there's likely to be plenty of space for a small table and shelves. If you have an alcove which is free for use, a good carpenter will be able to create a cupboard that will open on to a shelf that can be hidden away. This is a great option if you're lacking in space and don't want your working area to impose on your living space. Spare bedrooms can very easily be multitasked – a small table and storage and you've got an office space available

THIS PAGE: Even a small corner can be adapted to provide an attractive and nicely lit workspace area. OPPOSITE: Pretty file boxes, wire pigeonhole shelving and a vintage desk provide storage while the art enhances the space.

Storage and Display

Keeping my workspace clear of chaos and multiple paper stacks is the bane of my life. Over the years, I have spent much time working out ways that I can keep my office a place of calm and serenity and not somewhere that my son watches YouTube and leaves empty crisp packets and half-drunk glasses of juice. Sigh. Anyway, it's taken a good while to reach the point where I've managed to perfect my storage and display solutions, and I'm pretty pleased with them. The aim, of course, has always been to create a room that is as resourceful and practical as it is nice to look at, and I like to think that I've nailed it.

When you're planning out your office space, the first stop is storage. Everyone has to have somewhere for the tax files of doom, the copious bills and the passports and driving licences that you can NEVER find when you need them. In my own space, I used two IKEA sideboard units that I'd had for years and were past their prime and upcycled them, painting them, wallpapering the shelves and adding new handles before placing them one on top of the other. An easy and effective update, which successfully manages to hide away all those essentials that need not be seen.

OPPOSITE: *Simple wire-box shelving is perfect for displaying books and plants.* *THIS PAGE* above: *A wall-mounted magazine rack is an excellent space saver.* **Below**: *A metal filing cabinet doubles up as display space.*

Next up, look at your wall space. You need to utilize every inch of this to the maximum advantage. Corkboard is a great place to start. Cover a whole wall with floor tiles (carpet glue spray is perfect for this purpose) and you'll have a floor-to-ceiling board to which you can pin reminders, photos, inspiration and favourite memories. Or create a chalkboard by painting the wall in magnetic blackboard paint, a handy in-your-face diary so that you don't forget the important things. Both of these work really well as focal points in your room and tick the box for being practical yet nice to look at. Your rooms need to make you happy and your office is no exception.

Shelves are an essential in any office space – add them wherever you have spare wall space. It's simply not possible to overkill the storage. Make them stand out by using attractive solutions such as basketware and printed boxes so that your storage is a focal point in itself. Picture ledges have the double whammy of enabling you to create a display while not taking up the space area of a fully blown shelf. Display relevant or favourite books and prints; use trailing greenery to bring the outside in. Style your desk as you would any other surface in your home. Add plants, pretty storage pots and good task lighting so that your working space encourages you to, well, work. And, finally, create the perfect 'let's get down to work and stop the scrolling and procrastinating' ambience by keeping a scented candle going to promote that sense of calm and zen so that you can be as productive as humanly possible. We can but try.

OPPOSITE: *Plants are an excellent way to add both colour and interest to an office space.* **THIS PAGE:** *A wall of cork tiles works brilliantly as an ever-changing display.*

OUTSIDE

Whether you have a balcony, a small backyard or a fully fledged garden, making the most of your outside space is an essential part of creating a home that works for you. We're not always, of course, blessed with the most clement weather so planning is key when you're working out how best to utilize what you've got. I'm historically not the greatest gardener and have been known, most years, to forget to 'winterize' the garden. This basically means putting all your seating and accessories away in preparation for colder, wetter times and not ruining all your garden furniture, so that when you return after winter you don't find your cushions covered in algae.

This year, I ventured out to find our outside space looking like the Marie Celeste – filthy BBQ complete with tongs, piles of dead leaves, half-used candles, broken hanging pots, baskets filled with spider-infested throws and a bamboo plant sitting in a full pot of fetid water. It was as if we'd walked away halfway through a party and not gone back. Which is basically what we had done, if I'm being honest. I always tell myself that failing to prepare is preparing to fail and then always,,, Fail. There's always next year.

The first thing to do when planning your outside space is to assess the situation. From experience, I can confirm that it matters not a jot how awful you think it looks, it can absolutely and most definitely be improved. As always, look at the bones of what you have. Patios and decking can be transformed with a jet wash and a stiff brush, and if they're past their prime, look at exterior paints to prolong their life. Even the most horrible-looking patio slabs can be improved with a good-quality floor paint. The same applies to your walls and fences. If you hate the colour of the new brick or wooden panels in your back garden, get out the paintbrush. You might feel unsure when it comes to making such a big visual change, but remember this – if you really don't like it now, the chances are any update will improve what you've got. Have confidence in yourself. Greenery really pops against black walls, with the added bonus of a deep colour hiding any faults and horrible bits. White can make your space – whether you have a balcony or a patio – feel like the Mediterranean and can be teamed with luxe colour to give you that summertime feel. Or if you have a passion for the statement wall, try a bright tone that will create an impact.

Next, look at your furniture. If you're going to invest, it's a good idea to find pieces that you can use both indoors and outdoors so that you can make the very most of them when the weather isn't so warm. It's tempting to put your cash into a big outdoor set but if it's not usable for six months of the year, how good an investment is it? You'll find that much of your interior furniture can be perfectly multitasked in an outdoor environment when the weather is clement, particularly if you have a covered outdoor space such as a pergola, lean-to or shaded balcony. Add to what you've got with cushions and throws for when the sun goes down, and style your outdoor lounging area the same as you would your indoor space. Treat your outdoor space as an outdoor ROOM.

OPPOSITE: It doesn't matter whether your outside space is a compact balcony, a patio or a spacious garden, it's important to make the most of every inch of what you have.

Add potted plants. If you have a spare wall or fence area that's dead space, use scaffold planks to create a plant wall. It's a cheap way to create a focal point in your garden, or on a patio or balcony, and the styling possibilities are endless. Again, this is all part of the outdoor room concept – you have shelves indoors so why not outdoors? Go for evergreens in planters that don't need to be swapped out annually. Try ivies, succulents and hardy trailers that will grow and last if you're looking for good coverage. And push your boundaries to try something new – I've planted some vegetables from seeds this year in a wooden tray and it's really satisfying to watch them grow. If you don't have wall space, upcycle a shelving unit in outdoor-friendly paint so that you can stack it with greenery.

OPPOSITE: A covered area means that your use of the space isn't weather dependent. THIS PAGE: Use different textures of planter for your outdoor pots and group them for impact.

THIS PAGE clockwise from top left: Bring the inside out; encaustic tiles add contrast; and textiles add pattern and colour. *OPPOSITE*: Festoon lighting strung across the courtyard creates an ambient and welcoming space.

Zone your space by dividing it into areas. Work out what you are going to be using it for and focus on what can go where. Set a space aside for the BBQ and create a cosy living area – firepits are great for bringing the warmth when it's a bit chilly, plus they're a perfect social focal spot. Layer rugs and mix textures such as bamboo and wicker to juxtapose the look and create a welcoming space to sit and relax. If you've got an outside table, use an outdoor rug beneath (polypropylene can be left outside pretty much year round as long as you're handy with the jet wash) to anchor the space and promote the perfect dining ambience. Make the seats comfortable with cushions and cosy blankets so that you can sit outside and socialize until the early hours. Bring out your favourite table and glassware to make every meal a special event.

And, finally, lighting is the icing on the cake of your outdoor room. Festoons have come on leaps and bounds in recent years and are now LED, which means not only do they last for ages but they also give off enough light so that you barely need any other light source. String them across your space, whether it be big or small and, before you know it, you'll feel as if you're relaxing in the South of France. Large Kilner or Mason jars are ideal to use as hurricane lamps to add the ambience and will give a soft warm glow to your dining display, or dot small drinking glasses with tea lights along your table. Simple and effective.

THIS PAGE above. *Patterned fabrics up the ante in this cosy corner.* **Below:** *A vintage tea trolley can be brought outside and multitasked.* OPPOSITE above: *Make the most of every inch of your space.* **Below:** *Tea lights bring a soft glow.* OVERLEAF: *An outdoor movie night is great fun and easy to set up.*

Guest Annex

When we came to view our house, it was empty. There was hardly anything in it – the owners had already moved out, the rooms were bare and there was tumbleweed in the hallway. There really is nothing better than viewing a house in this position – not only can you see the spaces for how they really are, so you can envisage what you can do with them, but also, most importantly, you can say exactly what you want with no fear of being rude. It had a separate garage, half of a converted barn (semi-detached with the neighbour) that was a storage room on the ground floor and a gym above. We bought the house, moved in and immediately flogged the gym equipment on eBay. Despite my husband being a gym addict, I am not. Years ago, I worked for StairMaster, an American exercise equipment brand that produced stepping machines. I spent many years explaining to people that I had no involvement with old people in stair lifts, a commonly assumed fact. I managed to go the full four years of employment without stepping on one once, an amazing feat considering I was completely surrounded by them in my workspace.

Anyway, we decided that we would set this newly vacated room up as a teen den – I painted it in blackboard paint, bought lots of bean bags and framed cool posters for the walls. It took less than two weeks and one party for it to be completely destroyed. When it comes to teen parties, I have always been of the opinion that 'if they're doing it here, they're not doing it elsewhere and I know about it'. However, I didn't quite anticipate how much they would be 'doing'. Think 15-year-olds arriving midwinter wearing no tights and Barbie-sized clothes, copious amounts of cider, hard-core grime music, crying girls and broken bannisters and you'd be on the right track. From this point on, I refused point-blank to enter the room unless in exceptional circumstances, such as fire or serious injury, and as a result it looked more like a crack den than the clean-cut hang-out zone that I'd intended it to be.

I soon realized that it didn't have to be like this. Living a fair distance from our family, it's not unusual for us to have five or six people staying at the same time and, with one guest room, we are always aware that we could actually do with a bit more space. The garage seemed the perfect conversion project, as it was already a usable area. The intention was to convert it into a self-contained annex, while halving the ground floor to maintain a storage space. The left-hand side would be shelved storage and the right-hand would comprise a shower room and entrance hall. Upstairs there would be a small kitchen area, a living space and a separate double bedroom. The aim was threefold: it would act as accommodation for friends and family; it would create a new and interesting area for me to work on brand projects; and we'd make the money back that we'd pay to extend the mortgage (in order to do the work) by renting it as an Airbnb at certain times of the year. But one of the main focuses of this build would be to utilize and make the most of a) what we already had and b) what we could create using basic materials. Here's where we added value and sustainability to the project without spending huge amounts of money.

OPPOSITE: Smoked glass windows were added to the original garage doors, which were then painted black.

The Basics:

The original wooden garage doors were past their prime but we wanted to bring them back to their former glory. We removed a panel from each and replaced with smoked glass, sanding down and repainting in black and adding gold hardware. Inside, we built a frame and used 50mm (2in) sheets of insulation, covering the whole lot with 6mm (¼in) MDF and painting to match. We made our own internal doors from 25mm (1in) MDF, which we painted black and added hardware, giving a simple door a luxe look. The exception was the shower room door for which we purchased a single glazed door and added fluted glass from a local glazier. I wanted to make the most of the light so instead of enclosing the stairs, we made a slatted bannister, which created a lovely bright space.

Shower Room:

This was a small room so in order to make the most of this windowless space, I kept it simple by using the same orange colour pop tile throughout, teamed with white walls. I wanted to incorporate a fully tiled worksurface 1970s style, with a slatted wood shelf beneath, so we built the frame with carcassing and moisture-resistant backer board. The same board was used to create a shower wall – easier to keep clean than a glass screen and fully tiled, therefore ensuring the colour flowed throughout the space. I added art by framing David Shrigley postcards in acrylic sleeves, which protected them from moisture and enabled me to swap them in and out if I wanted to change the look.

Storage:

As it was a small space, I wanted to include as much storage as possible. We made the most of the understairs area by building inset shelving from MDF within it, the perfect size for magazine storage. We used the bannister frame that was already there at the top of the stairs to do the same, creating an inset bookcase. I filled the shelves with vintage Penguin paperbacks that I'd found at a local charity sale, adding colour and character.

Kitchen:

Keen to keep costs down but also create something individual, we bought basic kitchen carcasses from a local DIY store and added moisture-resistant MDF cut to size to create the doors. Again, we added the luxe factor with gold handles and painted the doors in dark green. I wanted a solid wood worktop with matching floating shelf but this was out of the budget. Instead, we bought a 2m (6½ft) breakfast bar length of oak and cut the additional width to create the shelf – far more economical than buying separately. The shelf was fixed with strong struts in the wall to keep it secure.

Bedroom:

I really wanted to keep the space fairly clean and minimal in this room so I bought recycled tea crates to use as side tables. I added a wall light and an invisible book shelf each side, with a huge repurposed Moroccan-style rug beneath. Art from a local gallery added an individual touch, and black sliding doors meant that every inch of the room was usable.

Making the most of what we had, bringing in vintage furniture and multitasking when needed created an individual space with real impact. The hallway boasts a G Plan Fresco dressing table that has been repurposed as a desk space, teamed with a pale pink contemporary Flokk Design chair. I've reused favourite china and accessories from my own home, collating them into focal points and adding plants to bring the outside in. Clever storage and statement flooring, such as the jumbo terrazzo in the hallway and shower room, add interest while the art creates an ambience that is both interesting and welcoming. It's also warm as toast, thanks to the insulated updated garage doors, but with plenty of natural light coming from the smoked glass windows.

Clockwise from top: The bannister was
rebuilt as a storage alcove for books;
sliding doors create extra space in the
bedroom; and a round bamboo mirror is
a contrast to the square tiles.

RESOURCEFUL SOURCING

Making your spaces interesting and resourceful by adding thrifted and repurposed finds, alongside key investment pieces, is a surefire way to make your home work for you. Recycling preloved items will not only add beauty to your home, but is also a more sustainable and cost-effective choice.

THE JOY OF THRIFTING

I've always been addicted to upcycling and repurposing. The joy of giving an unloved item a new lease of life is truly exciting. Nowadays, we live in a consumer-led society where we are constantly bombarded with options for purchasing a new piece of furniture, but in reality, buying vintage can be a fabulous investment. It's easy to forget that the reason that these pieces are still around today is that they were made to last and

the quality is often unrivalled. Whether you give your vintage furniture a complete paint job or simply get out the polish, it's hugely satisfying to know that you're repurposing something and perpetuating the recycling process.

As the saying goes, one man's trash is another man's treasure and I'm ALL about the treasure. Previously discarded as uncool and boring, brown furniture is back with a vengeance and one of the reasons for this is that it's brilliantly made. Look for the dovetailed joints in the drawers which are a dead giveaway that it's quality – some of these pieces have been around for over 70 years. Check for marks and labels – you never know what you're going to find.

So why buy vintage? Well, firstly and most importantly, you are perpetuating the recycling process and furnishing your home sustainably by helping the environment – by choosing preloved furniture, you are stopping these items being landfilled. You're also often making your money go further. Vintage furniture can be far better made than something you would buy new from a store for twice the price. Buying second-, third- or even fourth-hand will make your own home stand out in a crowd by encouraging you to create your own, individual style. It's easy to be trend-led and matchy-matchy when it comes to decorating your space. Combining older furniture alongside newer pieces adds a cool and eclectic feel to your home. And, finally, you're giving back. Not only do you take home a piece of furniture that will add to the happiness of your home, but you are often

making an effective and worthy contribution to a charitable cause.

There is nothing more satisfying than bringing an old, unloved piece of furniture back to life and incorporating it successfully into your space. The best way to create a beautiful home that works for you is to juxtapose older pieces filled with history and memories alongside well-thought-out investment purchases. Winning.

*OPPOSITE: Browsing the aisles at my local thrift shop, Junk & Jewels. **THIS PAGE** clockwise from top left: Vintage bedding at The French House, York; thrifted accessories and art that can add character to your space; and mismatching brass candlesticks grouped to create impact.*

10

KEY VINTAGE BUYS

Crocheted Blankets

Always check out the textiles section when thrift shopping – often a nirvana of '80s duvet covers, net curtains and granny blankets. You never know what you'll find but look out for tablecloths, hand-crocheted folk blankets (a personal favourite) and bed covers.

Vases

From mid-century West German pottery to SylvaC plant pots, there's gold in them charity shop hills. Curate similarly colour-toned pieces for a display or start a collection – Glug water vases are fun to source and look great en masse. Always check the bases for maker's marks too.

Books

Books, books and more books. Stack them, style them, colour-code them – hell, even read them. An easy vintage buy but such a good one and a perfect example of repurposing and reusing. Old books are beautiful and add a layer of interest and personality to your home.

Art

Vintage prints are an excellent juxtaposition to modern art and typography in a gallery wall. Search for floral oils, old photographs and mid-century art, plus check out the picture frames, which can almost always be taken off and reused.

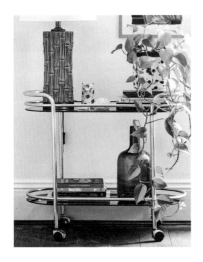

Drinks Trolleys

Truly a flexible vintage buy, the drinks trolley can be multipurposed throughout your home. Whether it's a classic tea and cake server or an eighties gold smoked glass original, these utilitarian beauties work just as well as side tables or home bars and are perfect for styling.

Bamboo Tables

Bamboo, wicker and rattan furniture may have been around for years, but it's eternally cool and translates brilliantly for modern living. Teamed with contrasting textures, it brings an eclectic edge to your room and can also be used outdoors during the summer months.

Glassware

Vintage glass is discarded in abundance and can be repurposed in your home to great effect. Dessert is so much prettier when presented in a cut-glass bowl, and why serve your prawn cocktail on a plate when you can use a vintage stemmed dish?

Tea Chests

Used to ship tea across the world, these chests are ideal for multitasking in your home as either furniture or an attractive alternative to traditional storage. The perfect dimensions for a bedside or living room side table, they're sturdy and practical and make your space unique.

Mid-Century Storage

The person who designed the mid-century sideboard knew what they were doing. Not only do they still look cool 60 years on, they are excellent for storing crockery, cutlery and even after-dinner games. Most importantly, they're nearly always equipped with a drinks cupboard.

Vintage Rugs

Don't rule out secondhand rugs. A faded vintage Persian runner is full of character and history – it may have lost pile but it still has years of use in it. There's a raft of revived Beni Ourain-style Moroccan rugs on the market that will add timeless appeal.

THRIFTING CHECKLIST

1. BE PREPARED

Looking for vintage treasure is an excellent way to spend a few hours. The best way to thrift shop is to make a day – or at least a morning – of it. List your shops of choice, plan your route and make sure you've got plenty of shopping bags for your finds. The early bird catches the worm, and all that.

2. OPEN YOUR MIND

The most exciting thing about thrifting is that you never know what you will find so shop with an open mind. Allow your eye to be drawn and find pieces that appeal to you and fit your aesthetic. I like to think that the preloved items I find in thrift shops have called to me in an 'it's fate' kind of way. My husband disagrees.

3. SHOP CLEVER

Think beyond the obvious – that floral print might not be your vibe but the glorious gold frame that it's inside may work wonderfully with a family photograph. And a vintage vase could multitask brilliantly as a container on your dressing table.

4. START A COLLECTION

I have a cupboard full of thrift-sourced glassware, from crystal wine glasses through to Babycham saucers, that I've bought slowly over time. Having a collection in mind means you can pick up items individually as and when you see them and then, before you know it, you'll have a full set.

5. PERUSE THE FABRICS

Vintage textiles are often overlooked but can be transformed with a quick wash and a laundry spray. Old duvet covers and sheets can multipurpose as tablecloths, or use the fabric for your own sewing projects. Personally, I can never leave a hand-crocheted blanket behind in a thrift shop – they're heirloom pieces, in my book.

6. QUALITY CHECK

Always check the markings on the base when you are looking at vintage china – you never know what you will find. One man's trash is another man's treasure. The same applies to vintage furniture – always pull out the drawers to check if they are dovetailed (a sign of quality) and check the back of the piece for maker's marks.

ONLINE SOURCING

Yes, I get it. For some, trawling through musty shelves and fighting their way through the crowds for the best thrift finds isn't their bag. If you fall into this category yet have a passion for recycling and repurposing, online thrifting is the answer to your prayers. The pages of the online auction sites are the Thelma to my Louise, the Kanye to my Kim; an enabler to achieve my decor goals. Their pages taunt me regularly with mid-century furniture bargains that start at 99p ($1) and go up to £800 ($1,000) within about three seconds. One minute it's yours and you're home free; next minute somebody hunched over their iPad in Birmingham is going in with three seconds to go and outbidding you. It's a dasher of dreams but, gosh, it's addictive.

From tubular 1960s brown leather Pieff loungers to vintage tea trolleys, from boho Peacock chairs to G Plan coffee tables, my home has been filled with countless fabulous auction wins and purchases and, let's face it, some absolute rubbish. I'll never forget the cocktail cabinet, picked up on Gumtree selling site for a fiver, only to open the doors to be accosted by cigarette fumes strong enough to knock me out. Undeterred, I bleached it, sprayed it with disinfectant and painted it in oil eggshell but still the aura of eau de Marlboro remained. I admitted defeat and listed it on a Freecycle site with full details of its scented detractions. But, as I've said before, one man's trash is another man's treasure – it was collected within two hours and went off to its new home in the sun. Well, North Yorkshire.

It's impossible not to find something to bid on or purchase when scouring the online havens of the secondhand. Know what you are looking for, use clear search words and set yourself a budget – it's easy to get carried away. My favourite searches are retro and vintage furniture – many is the time I've gone down a rabbit hole of 1970s sofas and coffee tables and come out with no idea of how I'm going to get them from Mid Glamorgan to York. Be wary of location – I always set the distance to within 30 miles, unless I am intent on a particular purchase, in which case I'll get quotes from a courier company prior to bidding. Think out of the box when it comes to search terms. I once won a vintage red leather Natuzzi corner sofa in perfect condition (original price around £5,000/$6,500) for £400 ($520) which had no one bidding on it but me, simply because they'd taken a shocking photo and just listed it as a red sofa. Hours and hours of fun. Oh, and an absolute money pit.

Look for local selling sites that have no selling fees – Facebook Marketplace, Gumtree and Craigslist are perfect for this purpose and you'll often find pieces where the buyer wants a quick sale and collection. If you're eBay bound, make sure you check out sellers' ratings and feedback so that you can buy safely and in confidence that they're a respected user.

OPPOSITE: Head to online marketplaces such as eBay if you're looking to add to your home. Know what you are looking for and what you are prepared to pay so that you don't get carried away.

GIVING BACK

So you've had a room reshuffle. You've worked out what you love, what you don't love and you have a big pile of things that are surplus to requirements. What to do with them? You have a few options but primarily, the main focus is to sell or donate. If it's a large item such as furniture and you've got your eye on something fresh for your home, then follow the sell-to-buy concept and use the money made to invest in the new. I've used this on many an occasion to justify a purchase.

Donate your unwanted items to charity. The first and most important reason for giving back is that you are perpetuating the recycling process. In the UK, the abundance of charity shops makes donating your items easy, which not only ensures that they will be repurposed and loved in another home, but that the charity will be benefiting financially from your actions. And if you buy FROM the charity shops and stores, everyone is a winner, as you will be adding something cool to your home while supporting a cause and repurposing at the same time. Perfect.

Find your local Community Furniture Store. Most areas will have units such as these, which are set up to take donations and resell to purchasers at two different prices – one if you are on benefits (thus helping lower income families to furnish their homes) and one if you are not. These facilities will often collect free of charge and also deliver free of charge as long as you are within a sensible distance. And, of course, all money spent goes toward keeping this service going, so you're

giving back to the community. Seek out charities such as Emmaus, if you're in the UK, that are dedicated to helping the homeless. Not only do they have fund-raising furniture stores nationwide to raise money for the cause, they also work with companions to run workshops on how to upcycle and bring unloved and damaged pieces back to life. It's a way of teaching new skills at the same time as helping those in need.

OPPOSITE: *Seek out your local thrift shops, house-clearance warehouses and charity shops so that you have a route to give back at the same time as adding new finds.*

Directory of Resources

ONLINE THRIFTING

eBay ebay.co.uk
Facebook Marketplace
facebook.com/marketplace
Freecycle freecycle.org
Gumtree gumtree.com
Preloved preloved.co.uk
Shpock shpock.com

CHARITIES*

Age UK ageuk.org.uk
Barnardos barnardos.org.uk
British Heart Foundation
bhf.org.uk
Cancer Research
cancerresearchuk.org
Childrens Society
childrenssociety.org.uk
Community Furniture Stores
communityfurniturestore.co.uk
Crisis crisis.org.uk
DEBRA debra.org.uk
Emmaus emmaus.org.uk
FARA faracharityshops.org
Headway headway.org.uk
Islamic Relief UK
Islamic-relief.org.uk
Marie Curie mariecurie.org.uk
Mind mind.org.uk
Oxfam oxfam.org.uk
PDSA pdsa.org.uk
Salvation Army
salvationarmy.org.uk

Save The Children
savethechildren.org.uk
Scope scope.org.uk
Sense sense.org.uk
Shelter England.shelter.org.uk
Sue Ryder sueryder.org
The Red Cross
redcross.org.uk
Traid traid.org.uk
YMCA ymca.org.uk

*Local hospice shops are also
a great place to pick up
preloved gems.

ONLINE VINTAGE TRADERS AND AUCTIONS

1st Dibs 1stdibs.com
Century 20 Design Show
centurytwenty.com
Decorative Collective
decorativecollective.com
Discover Vintage Interiors
discovervintageinteriors.co.uk
Etsy UK etsy.co.uk
Junk Deluxe junkdeluxe.co.uk
Kernow Furniture
kernowfurniture.co.uk
Mayfly Vintage
mayflyvintage.co.uk
Mosey Home moseyhome.co.uk
Pamono pamono.co.uk
RE-found Objects
re-foundobjects.com

Retro Vintage
retrovintageonline.co.uk
Retrouvius retrouvius.com
Scaramanga scaramangashop.co.uk
The French House – London
thefrenchhouse.co.uk
The French House – York
York.thefrenchhouse.co.uk
The Old Cinema
theoldcinema.co.uk
The Sale Room the-saleroom.com
Vinterior vinterior.co
Vintique vintiquelondon.co.uk
Virtual Vintage Fair
virtualvintagefair.co.uk

VINTAGE FAIRS

AS Fairs asfairs.com
B2B Events b2bevents.info
Festival Of Vintage
festivalofvintage.co.uk
IACF Antique Fairs iacf.co.uk
Jaguar Antique Fairs
jaguarfairs.com
Judy's Vintage Fair
judysvintagefair.co.uk
Modern Shows modernshows.com

HIGH STREET FAVOURITES

Anthropologie anthropologie.com
Dunelm dunelm.com
French Connection
frenchconnection.com

H&M Home hm.com

Habitat habitat.co.uk

Heals heals.com

Homesense homesense.com

IKEA ikea.co.uk

John Lewis johnlewis.com

JYSK jysk.co.uk

Liberty libertylondon.com

Ligne Roset ligneroset.co.uk

Loaf loaf.com

Made made.com

Maisons Du Monde
maisonsdumonde.com

Marks & Spencer
marksandspencer.com

Oliver Bonas oliverbonas.com

SCP scp.co.uk

Selfridges selfridges.com

Skandium skandium.com

Soho Home sohohome.com

The Conran Shop
conranshop.co.uk

The White Company
thewhitecompany.com

West Elm westelm.co.uk

Zara Home zarahome.com

HOMEWARES

Aida aidashoreditch.co.uk

Aram Store aram.co.uk

Att Pynta attpynta.com

Cox & Cox coxandcox.co.uk

Cult Furniture cultfurniture.com

Divine Savages
divinesavages.com

Earl of East earlofeast.com

Eleanor Bowmer
eleanorbowmer.co.uk

Goodhood goodhoodstore.com

Graham & Green
grahamandgreen.co.uk

Hilary & Flo hilaryandflo.co.uk

Homeplace homeplace.co.uk

Inside Store LDN
insidestoreldn.com

Kin Home kinhome.co

La Redoute laredoute.co.uk

Lillian Daph lilliandaph.co.uk

Lucy Tiffney lucytiffneyshop.com

Mad Atelier mad-atelier.com

Made in Design
madeindesign.co.uk

Margaux Home
margauxhome.co.uk

Milk Home milkhomeuk.com

Moxon moxon.london

Muck N Brass mucknbrass.com

Nest nest.co.uk

New Tribe anewtribe.co.uk

Nordic House nordichouse.co.uk

Polkra polkra.com

Poppy & Honesty
poppyandhonesty.com

Quirk & Rescue
quirkandrescue.com

Resident residentstore.co.uk

Rockett St George
rockettstgeorge.co.uk

Rose & Grey Interiors
roseandgrey.co.uk

Southwood Living
southwoodliving.co.uk

Sunday & Story
sundayandstory.com

The Basket Room
thebasketroom.com

The Curious Dept
curiousdepartment.com

The Hambledon
thehambledon.com

The Loft & Us theloftandus.com

Unlimited Shop UK
unlimitedshop.co.uk

Violet & Thistle
violetandthistle.com

WA Green wagreen.co.uk

Wolf & Badger wolfandbadger.com

LIGHTING

Bag & Bones bagandbones.co.uk

Buster & Punch
busterandpunch.com

David Hunt Lighting
davidhuntlighting.co.uk

Dowsing & Reynolds
dowsingandreynolds.com

Festive Lights festivelights.co.uk

Iconic Lights iconiclights.co.uk

Light Up North lightupnorth.com

Original BTC originalbtc.com

Pooky Lights pooky.com

PAINT, PAPER, WALLPAPER, FABRICS AND FLOORS

Amtico amtico.com

Anna Hayman
annahaymandesigns.com

Annie Sloan anniesloan.com

Axminster Carpet
axminster-carpet.co.uk

B&Q diy.com

Bert & May bertandmay.com

Ca Pietra capietra.com

Cole & Son cole-and-son.com

Designers Guild
designersguild.com

Earthborn earthbornpaints.co.uk

Farrow & Ball farrow-ball.co.uk

Fibre Flooring fibreflooring.com

Graham & Brown
grahambrown.com

Little Green Paint Co
littlegreen.com

Otto Tiles ottotiles.co.uk

Poodle & Blonde
poodleandblonde.com

Romo romo.com

Style Library stylelibrary.com

Woodchip & Magnolia
woodchipandmagnolia.co.uk

ONLINE ART

Ace Club Art aceclub.art
Art of Protest Gallery
artofprotestgallery.com
Blank White Space
blankwhitespace.co.uk
Curious Egg curiousegg.com
GFDA gfda.co
Goldmark Atelier
goldmarkatelier.com
Jealous Gallery
jealousgallery.com
King & McGaw
kingandmcgaw.com
Liberty Gallery
liberty-gallery.com
Nelly Duff nellyduff.com
One Off To 25 oneoffto25.com
Print Club London
printclublondon.com
Pure Evil Gallery
pureevilgallery.com

INDEPENDENT ARTISTS

Anthony Burrill
anthonyburrill.com
Sarah Maple sarahmaple.com
Charlie Evaristo Boyce
charlieevaristoboyce.co.uk
Kavel Rafferty
kavelrafferty.bigcartel.com
Daisy Emerson
daisyemerson.com
Amy Beager amybeager.com
Sharon Walters londonartist1.com
Michelle Thompson
michellethompsonart.
  bigcartel.com
Adam Hemuss hemussart.com
Benjamin Murphy
benjaminmurphy.info
Shuby shuby.co.uk

Jo Peel jopeel.com
Jody Barton jodybarton.co.uk
Kin & Castle kinandcastle.com
Joanna Ham joannaham.com
Dave Buonaguidi
realhackneydave.com
Heath Kane heathkane.co.uk
David Shand printclublondon.com
Gayle Mansfield
gaylemansfield.co.uk
Sadie Tierney sadietierney.co.uk
Keri Bevan keribevan.com
Anna Marrow
annamarrow.squarespace.com
Babak Ganjei
babakganjeiworks.com
Diane Hill dianehill.co.uk
Margo McDaid
etsy.com/shop/margomcdaidart
Hannah Carvell
hannahcarvell.com
Amy Carter theartincarter.co.uk
Daniel Wooding
danwoodingacrylicart.com
Donk donklondon.bigcartel.com
Age Of Reason
age-of-reason-studios.com
Ros Shiers ros-shiers.com
Laetitia Rouget laetitiarouget.com
Caroline Hoy
etsy.com/uk/shop/hoypottery
James Brown jamesbrown.info
Tipperley Hill tipperleyhill.com
Ali Joe Designs alijoedesigns.com
Sandra Isaksson
sandraisaksson.com
Melanie Tong
melanietongpainting.com
Simon Wilson sifabricate.com
Beau & Badger
beauandbadger.co.uk
The Connor Brothers
theconnorbrothers.com
Alex Sickling alexsickling.co.uk

Lale Guralp laleguralp.com
Victoria Neave inpolife.com
Ces McCully cesmccully.com
Stella Vine stellavine.bigcartel.com
Rachel Louise Lee
rachellouiselee.co.uk
Ben Allen benallenart.com
Dan Cimmermann
dancimmermann.com
Ali Miller alimiller.co.uk

USA

VINTAGE SOURCING

AptDeco aptdeco.com
Chairish chairish.com
Craigslist craigslist.org
Dobbin St Vintage
dobbinstcoop.com
Estate Sales estatesales.net
Everything But The House
ebth.com
OfferUp offerup.com

HOMEWARE STORES

Crate & Barrel
crateandbarrel.com
Floyd Home floydhome.com
Homesense us.homesense.com
Jayson Home jaysonhome.com
One Kings Lane onekingslane.com
Pottery Barn potterybarn.com
Williams Sonoma
willliamssonoma.com

Canada

VINTAGE SOURCING

Aberfoyle Antique Market
aberfoyleantiquemarket.com
Kijiji kijiji.ca

Leslieville FleaMarket
leslievilleflea.com
Salvation Army Thrift Store
thriftstore.ca
Talize talize.com

HOMEWARE STORES

CB2 cb2.ca
Homesense homesense.ca
Pottery Barn potterybarn.ca
Urban Barn urbanbarn.com
West Elm westelm.ca

Australia

VINTAGE SOURCING

Gumtree gumtree.com.au
Sacred Heart Mission
sacredheartmission.org
Salvos Stores salvosstores.com.au
St Vincent De Paul Society
vinnies.org.au

HOMEWARE STORES

Adairs adairs.com.au
Bed Bath & Table
bedbathntable.com.au
Early Settler earlysettler.com.au
Freedom freedom.com.au
Pottery Barn potterybarn.com.au

New Zealand

VINTAGE SOURCING

Avondale Market
avondalesundaymarket.co.nz
Browns Bay Market
brownsbaymarket.co.nz
Op Shops Directory
nzopshops.co.nz

Riccarton Market
riccartonmarket.co.nz
Trademe trademe.co.nz

HOMEWARE STORES

A&C Homestore
achomestore.co.nz
Citta cittadesign.com
Father Rabbit fatherrabbit.com
The Design Store
thedesignstore.co.nz

Singapore

VINTAGE SOURCING

Carousell sg.carousell.com
Hock Siong hocksiong.com.sg
Journey East journeyeast.com
Junkies Corner
junkiescorner.com
Noden nodenhome.com

HOMEWARE STORES

Affordable Style Files
affordablestylefiles.com
Bungalow 55
thebungalow55.com
Crate & Barrel
crateandbarrel.com.sg
Maissone maissone.com
Taylor B taylorbdesign.com

*With many thanks to those who
helped me compile these listings:
Borja De Maqua, Evie Kemp,
Ball & Claw Vintage, Jan Skacelik,
Emma Jane Palin, Abigail Gordon,
Annabel Kerman, Sam Head, Marie
Hughes and Mary Lou Stirling-Knight.*

ADDITIONAL PHOTOGRAPHY

Kyle Books would like to thank the
following photographers and organisations
for their kind permission to reproduce the
photographs in this book:

Alamy Stock Photo Glasshouse Images 97.
Gap Interiors Bureaux 70; Julien
Fernandez – Architect www.thevenot-
architecte.com/www.octopuces.fr 55 above
left; David Giles 157 below; Tria Giovan –
Heiburg Cummings Design 61 below left;
Clive Nichols – Interior Designer Karen
Moore 167 below; Colin Poole 18;
Anya Rice 69; Rachael Smith 27 above left,
27 below right, 61 below right.
Getty Images Nadezda Todoresa/EyeEm
52 below.
Keith Stephenson Moordale wallpaper
by Mini Moderns 52 above; Quirky B
Honeycomb rug by Alternative Flooring 58.
Unsplash Kari Shea 154.

All other photography: Brent Darby /
Octopus Publishing Group Ltd.

With thanks also to the two thrift shops
photographed in this book:
Junk & Jewels York
www.junkandjewelshouseclearance.co.uk
@junk_and_jewels_and_more
The French House York
www.york.thefrenchhouse.co.uk
@thefrenchhouseyork

Index

UK/US GLOSSARY
charity shops – resale shops
cutlery – silverware
crisps – potato chips
drinks trolley – bar cart
duvet – comforter
first floor – second floor
ground floor – first floor
hob – cooktop
sideboard – baseboard
sweet shop – candy store
tea trolley – tea wagon
terraced house – row house
tights – pantyhose
trolley – cart
wardrobe – closet

Acknowledgments

When we moved to our home in York and I started documenting my room updates by posting some shoddy and extremely average photography via my Instagram feed, I never dreamed that five years later I would be writing a book. Social media gets a lot of flack but one of the huge benefits of Instagram is that it not only inspires creativity, it brings together like-minded people.

Thank you to Dee Campling who was my first 'real life' social media friend and my styling workshop partner in crime. To Bianca Hall, whose home is featured in the book, who I can always rely on to have exactly the same opinion as me and makes excellent cocktails. To my friends who love a cushion and a paint colour just as much as I do and who inspire me daily: Katty Patterson, Malcolm Begg, Emma Jane Palin, Kerry Lockwood, Melanie Lissack, Olivia Edwards-Silk and Kate Watson-Smyth.

To Karen Watson, who is always up for a charity shop trawl and messages me whenever she sees something I'd like on Gumtree. To my local friends who have tolerated my ever-changing plans (and inability to drink Prosecco): Sarah Jane Grey, Sharon Reid, Sam Humble, Charlotte Sweeting, Ruth Webber and Pandora Maxton. To Sam Head, Shiv Davies and Jane Walne for maintaining our friendship from afar, even though I've been hopeless at it. To Emma Garcia, whose own books inspired me to give it a go (and whose writing is comedy gold) and to Craig Humble for expanding my art knowledge so that sometimes I look as if I know what I'm talking about. To Mike Grey, who built me a barn good enough to make it into the *Telegraph* and hardly complained at all. To Marie Hughes, who is far and away the most inspirational person that I know, and Milo Hughes, who is both the bravest and cleverest child I have ever met.

To my sister Annabel who is just like me, but make it fashion. To my mum Sue, brother James and all my extended family for not really understanding what my job is most of the time but supporting me anyway. To my husband Joe, who is always there for me with (often unsolicited but usually pertinent) advice. To my amazing kids Ella, Max and Leo, who have put up with me looking at my phone 99 per cent of the time for the last four years and have finally stopped scoffing when I put #shelfie.

To Joanna Copestick for believing that I could write a book, Brent Darby for making my house look much neater than it actually is, Emilie Fournet for allowing us into her beautiful home, Florence Filose for putting up with my endless emails, and Rachel Cross for her amazing design skills. To Melanie Sykes, Rachel Khoo and Jess Doyle for writing such lovely endorsements.

And, most of all, thank you to everyone who has read my blog, followed me on Instagram, commented and subscribed over the last four years, without whom I wouldn't be writing this now. I appreciate your support SO MUCH. Please keep showing me your projects and resourceful tips by using the hashtag #resourcefulliving.